A Rainbow Book

Seminole Views

*A Postcard Panorama
of America's Only
Unconquered Tribe*

EMMETT H. L. SNELLINGS, JR.

Rainbow Books, Inc.
FLORIDA

Library of Congress Cataloging-in-Publication Data

Snellings, Emmett H. L., 1942-
  Seminole views : a postcard panorama of America's only unconquered tribe / Emmett H.L. Snellings, Jr. — 1st ed.
    p. cm.
  Includes bibliographical references and index.
  ISBN 1-56825-101-7 (hardcover : alk. paper)
 1. Seminole Indians—Florida—History—Pictorial works. 2. Seminole Indians—Florida—Social life and customs—Pictorial works. 3. Florida—History—Pictorial works. 4. Florida—Social life and customs—Pictorial works. I. Title.
  E99.S28S645 2007
  975.9004'973859—dc22
                              2007015170

Seminole Views: A Postcard Panorama of America's Only Unconquered Tribe
© 2008 by Emmett H. L. Snellings, Jr.

ISBN 10: 1-56825-101-7
ISBN 13: 978-1-56825-101-1

Published by
Rainbow Books, Inc.
P. O. Box 430, Highland City, FL 33846-0430

Editorial Offices

(863) 648-4420
RBIbooks@aol.com • www.RainbowBooksInc.com

Permissions
See pp. 217–218.

All rights reserved. No part of this book may be reproduced or transmitted in any form or by any means, electronic or mechanical (except as follows for photocopying for review purposes). Permission for photocopying can be obtained for internal or personal use, the internal or personal use of specific clients, and for educational use, by paying the appropriate fee to

Copyright Clearance Center
222 Rosewood Dr.
Danvers, MA 01923
U.S.A.

Disclaimer: Many of the old Tribal customs mentioned in the text are not practiced today. Oral history and recollections of interviewees can, at times, be fallible. People may remember events and other people somewhat differently from the way they actually were, as each person has his or her own interpretation of such things.

All photos are by the author, unless otherwise credited,
and all cards are from the Snellings Collection, unless otherwise credited.

The paper used in this publication meets the minimum requirements of the American National Standard for Information Sciences—Permanence of Paper for Printed Library Materials, ANSI Z39.48-1984.

First edition 2008
12 11 10 09 08 07   5 4 3 2 1

Dedicated in loving memory to Louise Blakely Snellings, whose sustaining love for the author was and is ever present, and her help in the production of this book was invaluable. In her, the Seminole Indians had a great admirer, and the warmth of her personality resulted in treasured friendships among the Tribe. She will be forever remembered, not only as a wonderful wife, but also as one who spread untold joy and happiness to the many lives that she touched.

Louise
(Snellings Photo)

Louise with the Young Cypress Family

Louise (far left) is pictured as a little girl of about seven or eight years old with Mitchell, David, Patsy and Mary Francis Fewell Cypress. Even at that early age she was interested in all things Native American. (Courtesy of Catherine Blakely.)

"Many daughters have done virtuously but thou excellest them all."
—Proverbs 31:29

My very special thanks go to the *Seminole Tribe* of Florida for granting me the right to use the Tribal Council seal and all or any part of the *Seminole Tribune*'s material/photos and/or the right to describe and portray in whole or in part any events, episodes or biographical information of fiction/nonfiction about Seminole Indians as portrayed in the *Seminole Tribune*, as well as four photos of Mitchell Cypress, James Billie, Betty Mae Jumper and Genus Crenshaw.

Also, special thanks to my good friend Patrick Smith for writing the foreword to this book.

Thanks to Pineapple Press, Inc., for permission to use Betty Mae Jumper's legends, taken from *Legends of the Seminoles*, 1994, by Betty Mae Jumper and Peter B. Gallagher.

—Emmett H. L. Snellings, Jr.

The official colors of the Seminole Tribe and what they represent:

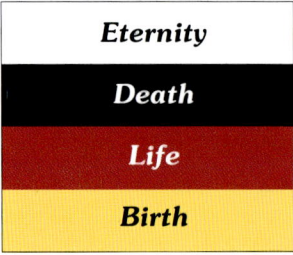

Contents

Foreword by Patrick D. Smith   ix

Preface   xi

Acknowledgments   xiii

Introduction   1

Chapter 1: Historical Background   3

Chapter 2: Wars and Warriors   9

Chapter 3: Historical Figures   23

Chapter 4: Black Seminoles   55

Chapter 5: Housing   59

Chapter 6: Traditional Food   65

Chapter 7: Clothing and Style   79

Chapter 8: Transportation   93

Chapter 9: The Everglades   105

Chapter 10: Medicine   121

Chapter 11: Religious Customs   129

Chapter 12: Legends   147

Chapter 13: Tourism   155

Chapter 14: Crafts   167

Chapter 15: Children   175

Chapter 16: Education   193

Chapter 17: Cattle Business   199

Chapter 18: All Things Seminole   203

References   213

Permissions   217

Index   219

About the Author   229

Foreword

I approached the chickee with caution — actually, a combination of caution, fear and apprehension. I could see an old man and a woman sitting on the ground beneath the palm fronds, sipping something from gourd dippers. Would they welcome me, and talk to me, or totally reject me? I expected to be rejected. I was.

The year was 1969, and I was just beginning what was to become a two-year quest to get inside the very heart and soul of the Seminoles. No one had done this before and put it into fiction, and I was beginning to think no one ever would.

This was long before such things as bingo and tourist attractions on their reservations brought great public attention to the Seminoles. They were virtually unknown, and most of them still lived the old ancestral way of life. They did not like or trust strangers — most especially "white strangers" — and when you study their past, who could blame them?

What I was searching for was background material to write a novel called *Forever Island*. In my research I found several books about Seminoles, but they were all written from a third person point of view — never in the Seminole's own words. Thus I knew I would have to get my information straight from the source. I wanted to know everything possible about their legends, superstitions, fears, religion, and their day-to-day life. I wanted to tell the story in this novel from a Seminole point of view, through Seminole eyes, not my own.

I finally did make friends with Seminoles who shared their lives with me. *Forever Island* was published in 1973, and was followed with another Seminole novel, *Allapattah*, and major roles for Seminoles in *A Land Remembered*.

Now comes along Emmett Snellings, Jr., with a FIRST PERSON! book about Seminoles — probably a first of its kind. What I would have given for such a book so many long years ago! It is a jewel — not just for historians or anthropologists or folklorists, but for anyone who wishes to take a fascinating excursion into the past of one of America's least known Native American tribes.

When Emmett first told me he was undertaking this project, I said, "Uh oh. Good luck." I doubted he would ever get so many Seminoles to talk about their ancestors as portrayed in postcards, but he did. He has accomplished a monumental task, and I salute him.

This book will be like fine wine — it will become more and more valuable as it ages. It just might be the only one in which the Seminoles talk about themselves, in the first person — stories told by them, not by someone else.

—Patrick D. Smith

Preface

Collecting Seminole postcards has been an ever increasing hobby in the United States over the last few decades, and the hobby of postcard collecting is called *deltiology*. There may be as many as a thousand postcard dealers across the country who sell Seminole cards. Postcard collecting in general is now the second largest hobby in the United States, second only to coin collecting. Old photo Seminole cards, originally costing just a few cents, may sell today for as much as $7,000 each. As Mr. Roberts told me:

"The height of the postcard era was like the height of the souvenir era, which was around the 1st World War. There were many postcards done then 'cause the focal point of Florida was the East Coast of Florida where all the tourists went. It was a total international thing, I mean not just all the United States went to Florida, it was like the American Riviera. A lot of Seminoles lived along the east coast, especially Ft. Lauderdale and Miami developed into a really hot-spot in the twenties, in the teens and twenties there were a lot of 'unique' Seminole pictures taken then. The hand colored postcards are a little rarer than most, 'cause they took a little extra detail."

—Larry Roberts, postcard dealer in Micanopy, Florida

Over the last decade, I have collected old Florida postcards. My interest in this segment of Florida memorabilia branched into a specialization in Seminole postcards because of my interest in all things that pertain to American Indian culture. At postcard shows and through various dealers across the U.S., I was able to amass one of the largest collections of these cards. In 1998 I decided to write this book using the old postcards (along with a few new ones) as visual entry points into the culture of Florida's Seminoles.

During the ten years that it took to finish this project, I encountered many difficulties to the task. The Seminoles want matters involving their history and culture to be preserved, but many don't want to talk about it — especially to a white man. Getting them to talk about their medicine is nearly impossible (though medicine man, Josie Billie, did cover this subject extensively with anthropologist William Sturtevant in the early 1950s).

Sometimes just getting them to keep appointments was a big task in itself, and I was "stood up" or kept waiting for long periods of time on many occasions. I was informed that such behavior is not only characteristic of them but was sometimes a test of your tenacity. Indians generally don't like people who are undetermined or weak of character. It's sort of a gauntlet that is laid down to "test your mettle."

In truth, most of the Seminoles don't care if you write about them or not. Nevertheless, author and Indians did get together eventually, and underneath the hard surface were usually kind and interesting people with varied concerns. The task of putting names with the faces on some of the old postcards required much time talking with the elders of the Tribe while they reflected upon the days of yesteryear.

Acknowledgments

The following people provided invaluable information and experiences for this book: James Billie, Mitchell Cypress, Jeanette Cypress, Sally Tommie, Danny Tommie, the late Jimmy O'Toole Osceola, Pat Diamond, the late Laura Mae Osceola, the late Annie Jimmie, Buffalo Tiger, Elaine Agilar, Louise Gopher, Stanlo Johns, Virginia Mitchell, Betty Mae Jumper, Mary Jane Storm, Susan Gillis, Billy Cypress, the late Regis Shiffbauer, Tommy Taylor, Bobby C. Billie, the late Susie Jim Billie, the late Henry John Billie, Frank Billie, the late Genus Crenshaw, Paul Buster, Joe Dan Osceola, Larry Roberts, Paul Bowers, John Micco, George Osceola, Geniva Shore, Marcia Greene, Guy LaBree, Josephine Motlow North, Travis Trublood, the late John K. Mayhon, William Osceola, Moses Jumper, Jr., and Swamp Owl.

Tribal Chairman, Mitchell Cypress

Tribal Chairman Mitchell Cypress
(Courtesy of the Seminole Tribe Chairman's Office)

Mitchell Cypress has been Chairman of the Seminole Tribe of Florida since 2003. He served as President of the Tribe's Board of Directors from 1995–2003. A personable yet strong man, he has supervised and directed in one way or another almost all phases of Tribal government, including such areas as education, culture, gaming, cattle, citrus and tobacco. Duties during his political career have included everything from passing Tribal resolutions to organizing the recording of gospel songs in his native tongue.

One thing that concerns Mitchell Cypress is something over which he has little, if any control. For many years the Everglades has been under siege from developers, large agricultural interests and recreational concerns.

"All along we've been saying save the Everglades, but during the '80s and '90s there was development all the way up to Route 27. Within the next 20 years there is not going to be such a thing as saving the Everglades; they're going to just jump all over and Naples and Miami are going to come together one day. Developers from the north and everybody from the north comes down here and they don't understand anyway, so the contractors get their money and fly back to New York. Money talks, money moves people. We are going to destroy the Everglades, birds, deer and alligators. One day the only thing we're going to see is in the zoo. Man is going to destroy his own world; that's happening now as far as the Everglades are concerned."

—*Mitchell Cypress*

Acknowledgments

Former Chairman, James Billie

Former leader of the Seminole Tribe of Florida, James Billie, was the Chairman from 1979–2003. During that time he did a great deal for the Seminoles, yet he is a modest man, often trying to shift the credit to other people. This Vietnam veteran, singer and songwriter, alligator wrestler, helicopter pilot, and teller of folk tales, is shrewd in his business dealings and commands respect among the other Tribes of North America. A formidable foe, as some have experienced, he is not unlike the famous warriors of yesteryear who preceded him.

James Billie, Former Tribal Chairman
(Courtesy of the *Seminole Tribune*)

"I didn't change anything. You know there are businessmen who stand out, who are really good statesmen, like Bob Graham and Buddy MacKay. But I was in the category of a hunter, and I'm still in that category. That's why you never see me looking like I'm a chief. I'm just old Jim Billie, the hunter. I used to provide food for the family, go out and kill deer and alligators, and bring meat for supper."

—*James Billie*

Assistant to the Chairman, Sally Tommie

Sally Tommie

As the Assistant to the Chairman of the Seminole Tribe of Florida, she conducts much of the Tribe's daily business. Sally Tommie was the first Seminole to become seriously interested in this book and was responsible for it being originally sponsored by the Seminole Tribe President's Office. This extremely busy lady has contributed much to the project with her advice, introductions, interviews, and infectious smile. A friendly yet savvy executive, she is an inspiration to all. As an experienced business woman, she is a most valuable assistant to the chairman. (Snellings photo)

Afatchkee School Teacher, Jeannette Cypress

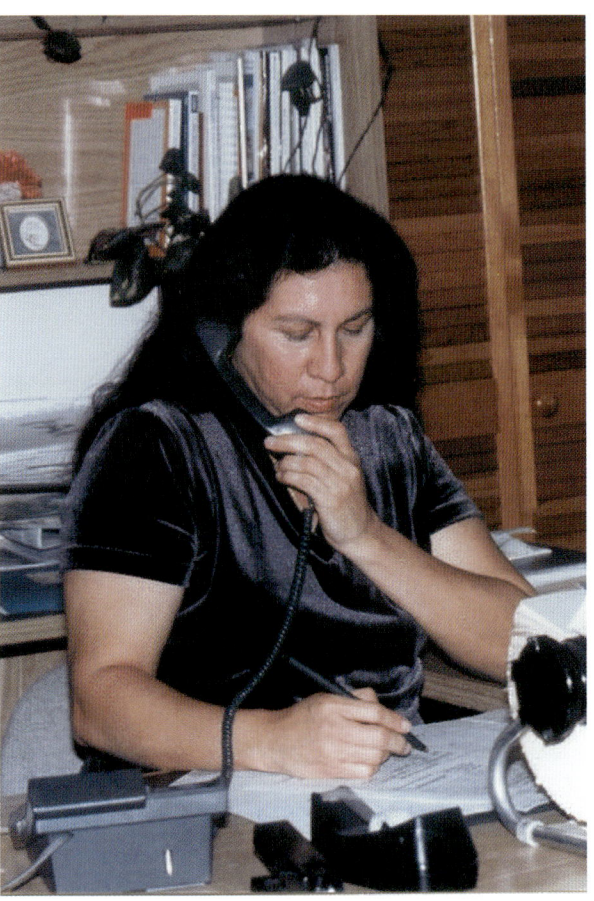

Jeannette Cypress

Jeannette has been indispensable to the production of this book. She exemplifies how well some Seminoles have adapted to the ways of the non-native world, yet she still holds to traditional Tribal ways. Perhaps the very thought of losing any part of her heritage makes her hold on to it that much harder. She wears many hats during a week's time: daughter, wife, mother, teacher, and believe it or not, grandmother. (Snellings photo)

Introduction

Che-han-ta-mo
(How are you?)

You are invited to come to the chickees, camps and reservations deep in *Pahayokee* (Everglades) and *Ashawechobee* (the Big Cypress Swamp) where the Seminole Indians have lived, fought wars, reared families and died since long before *Kanyuksa* (Florida) became part of the United States. Using postcards (some of which are nearly a century old) and related contemporary photographs as visual points of entry into the culture and history of the Tribe, the author will help the reader better understand this, the only unconquered Tribe of Indians in the United States.

Since establishing their first recorded settlements in North Florida in the mid-eighteenth century[1], Florida's Seminoles have been persecuted by other cultures. During the nineteenth century these Native Americans (not all Seminoles like that term) were removed from their homes by the U.S. government, cheated out of their land, and, in some cases, hunted and murdered.

Seminoles want their culture to be preserved, yet because of past experiences with non-natives, they are understandably reluctant to talk about it to outsiders. So-called altruistic

---

[1] Some historians believe the ancestors of modern-day Seminoles were living in what we now call Florida for many thousands of years.

efforts on the part of non-natives are often viewed with skepticism by many Tribal members. Consequently, interviews were often hard to get for this project and, in some cases, an interpreter had to be used to gather information. Many members of the Tribe are on what some of them laughingly call "Seminole time," which means they do things according to their own schedule — when they get ready. Patience was, therefore, a hard-won quality. Nevertheless, both author and Tribe, along with representatives from Independent Seminoles, have combined efforts in this book to provide some insight into this unique segment of Americana.

Seminoles are exciting people whose vivid past is relatively unknown to the general public. Since a cursory view of a postcard or photograph cannot capture the depth of this culture, commentary from various Tribal members is combined with research to give some of the history and background information behind each postcard and photograph. It is important to note that no single book can provide a comprehensive study of all phases of the complex world of the Seminole Indians. Historical texts about the Seminoles are often contradictory, so extra care was used to sort out the "facts." Filled with both humor and sadness, this book will help the reader to capture a glimpse of the heroic warriors, matriarchs, medicine men, Tribal leaders and both famous and infamous characters of yesteryear.

Let us now take this postcard journey along forgotten trails into the often mysterious world of the Seminole Indian.

Historical Background

The earliest recorded contact with the Natives of Florida occurred in 1513 when Ponce de Leon came to the territory near what is now St. Augustine, Florida.

Ponce de Leon most likely encountered the Timacuan Indians, but many Tribes inhabited the Florida territory prior to the arrival of European man, such as the Tocobaga, Matacumbe, Ais', Tequesta and others.

Arguably, the Seminole Tribe is comparatively young among the Indian Tribes of North America. They were originally a melting pot of groups that broke away from the Indians known as Creeks (both Upper and Lower Creeks) in Georgia and Alabama in the early eighteenth century. The English settlers called them Creeks because they were usually found near streams and rivers. Historians believe that the Lower Creeks crossed the border into Florida and mixed with other Tribes such as the Yemassee and possibly remnants of the Calusa, Timacuans, Apalachee and others. Some claim that Florida was devoid of Natives by 1710 and that the Indians we call Seminoles arrived after all these prior Native settlements had disappeared. But there are a few historians who claim that the ancestors of present day Seminoles have been in Florida for over 12,000 years.

Seminole Views

Herbert Jim

Some say he has Calusa features and is visual evidence of a Seminole/Calusa connection. (Snellings Photo)

"My grandmother was Addie Billie, great, great, granddaughter of Miami Billie, who was born in Georgia before the First Seminole War. She passed away at about 109 or 111 years of age, it is estimated. When she was born in the Everglades, she was a fourth generation Creek Indian. My grandfather was a very tall man, about 7 feet, and my uncles were also tall. My grandfather's name was Concho Billie. I don't know much about his background, only that he was born and raised in the Everglades. My mother was Alice Billie. She was also born in the Everglades.

"My great, great, great grandmother, Miami Billie, was about 5 years old when U.S. soldiers raided their camp. Her mother and father ran to the front of the house (log cabin) to hold back the soldiers, while her older brother escaped with Miami Billie through the back of the house and deeper into the Everglades.

"Miami remembered screaming and crying for her parents, while she watched them go down as they fought to protect their children. Miami and her brother met up with other bands of Seminoles. Her brother had to leave her with other family members because they needed him to help fight in the First Seminole War. My grandmother passed on this story to me. Miami Billie died at the tender age of 130.

"It is hard to say precisely where my family comes from. I can go back only so far before it becomes blurred. When the Creeks came to Florida there were many other tribes here. Some intermarried with us, while others fled deeper and deeper into the Everglades. They did not want to be discovered. I have heard stories of abandoned camps made by other natives who remain unknown to us. They say you would see camp fires at a distance, but by the time you got over there, the camp fire had moved to another location. It was like chasing a ghost in the Everglades."

—*Herbert Jim (as told to April Jim)*

Historical Background

Runaway Blacks from the plantations of the Carolinas and Georgia also mixed with the Tribe in the nineteenth century. In the twentieth century the Seminoles also began to intermarry with the whites. The blood in the veins of present day Seminoles descends from several races and other Native Tribes.

It has been said that an Englishman by the name of John Stuart, who was an Indian agent in 1771, was the first person to use the name "Seminole." White Americans eventually used the name to apply to all Indians who crossed into Florida from its northern border. The Spanish referred to Cowkeeper's band of early Seminoles as *"cimarrones,"* meaning "wild ones, separatists, renegades or runaways." Some say that the Upper Creek Indians pronounced it as "Seminoles," but others claim they said, *"isti siminoli"* or *"yat'siminoli,"* since the Muskogee (Maskoki) language of the Creeks has no "r" sound with which to pronounce *cimarrones*. The British later translated that into "Seminole." Some Seminoles do not like this name because they feel that it impugns their courage and steadfastness.

According to early naturalist, William Bartram (Puc-Puggy, as the Indians called him, meaning "flower hunter"), ". . . The visage, action, and deportment of the Seminole form the most striking picture of happiness in this life. Joy, contentment, love, and friendship, without guile or affectation, seem inherent in them or predominant in their vital principle, for it leaves them but with the last breath of life . . ."

Between 1740 and 1812, several villages of Lower Creek Indians were established in different areas of northern Florida. Some of these villages were located near present-day Tallahassee and Lake Miccosukee, and along the Suwanee River. Various Indian hunting parties explored the peninsula and traded with some Cuban fisherman on the western part of what was then Spanish territory. During that time the Seminoles made raids against the Spanish and the Apalachee Indians. From 1812 to 1820, increased pressure was placed on the Creek Indians from other Tribes and from white settlers moving west from coastal areas. They began to move into the Florida region from Georgia and Alabama. In the Seminole Wars (1816–18, 1835–42 and 1856–58), Seminoles often had to fight the Creeks, who were allied with the U.S. government, as well as the U.S. military. Some Seminoles say that there is no such thing as *three* Seminole wars; they say it was a continuing effort, and even today it continues in different ways.

Hitichi-speaking Lower Creeks came into the northern part of the territory of Florida (*ichi bomet* — the nose of the deer) in the early eighteenth century as the result of the enticements of the Spanish. These Lower Creeks may have mixed with the Apalachicola Indians already in that region. The Chiahas, who also spoke the Hitichi language, came to the panhandle of Florida near what is now the town of Miccosukee. The Tamothli Indians

> ". . . The knowledge of *ichi bomet* had been with our people for a long, long time. And *ichi bomet* was more than just the nose of the deer. It was that thin, long land where the soft, fresh breezes would blow over us and set our spirits free. When we all lived in that land, our spirits would be able to blow gently over into the other world, to the West, without even having to cross over physically. They knew about Florida, and our people were here for a long, long time before the white people think we were."
>
> —*Ronnie Jimmie*

were absorbed into this group. Muskogee-speaking Upper Creeks from Alabama came to Florida just northeast of Tampa Bay in 1767. Still other Upper Creeks (a group called Tallassees) settled in what had once been Apalachee territory in the panhandle of Florida. The Yuchi Indians came to West Florida in 1818 and eventually moved to what is now Volusia County. More Upper Creeks came to Florida in 1813–1814 as a result of the "Red-Stick War" (a war between the Upper and Lower Creeks) in Alabama, where troops under the command of Andrew Jackson intervened and killed over 800 Creeks. Even before the Seminole Wars, Jackson was practicing his debauchery.

Cowkeeper was the first distinguishable leader of those to whom we now refer as Seminoles, although there are several versions of how the Seminole Tribe came into existence. His band — known as the Alachua band — was a group of Lower Creek Indians, called the Oconees, who spoke the Hitchiti language. Later in the eighteenth century the Eufaula and the Upper Creeks, who spoke the Muskogee language, arrived in Florida. According to the famous explorer, William Bartram, Cowkeeper was leading his people toward the Atlantic Ocean. En route from the Oconee River area in Georgia in 1740, they settled near an area that is now called Payne's Prairie in Alachua County, Florida. Because of large swarms of mosquitoes, they moved to a camp called Cuscowilla near what is today called Micanopy. This village included several hundred people with many horses and cattle. There was also a considerable number of Yemassee (a tribe of Indians from the low country of South Carolina and southeastern Georgia) slaves at the village. Wooden houses were built in these early camps, not the chickees of the nineteenth and twentieth centuries.

Cowkeeper's group separated themselves from most of the rest of the Creek Indians who came to Florida, remaining somewhat loyal to the British instead of the Spanish, who governed Florida at that time. In 1763 Spain ceded Florida to England. Cowkeeper would not attend the meeting of the Creeks and the British at Picolata in 1765 when the rest of the

Historical Background

Creek leaders signed a treaty. Even in the stages of the infancy of the new Seminole identity, non-Indians were trying to take their land from them.

Cowkeeper's band was successful in raising cattle near their camp near what is today part of Payne's Prairie State Park (named after King Payne, the nephew of Cowkeeper and later a leader of the Seminoles). Americans greedy for land noticed this success and wanted the land occupied by the Seminoles. (That mindset has continued to this very day in one form or another.) Cowkeeper and his band maintained good relations with the British and there was relative calm until the United States overcame British authority at the end of the Revolutionary War. By 1784 both Spanish and American authorities recognized the Seminoles as separate from the Creeks.

Black slaves began to join the Seminoles in the early nineteenth century as they escaped the plantations of the Carolinas and Georgia. This was one of the main factors in the hostilities between white settlers and the Seminoles. Whites were constantly making raids across the Florida border from Georgia to capture the Black slaves who they claimed belonged to them.

Seminole Views

8

Interesting Reverse Sides of Seminole Cards from the Snellings Collection.

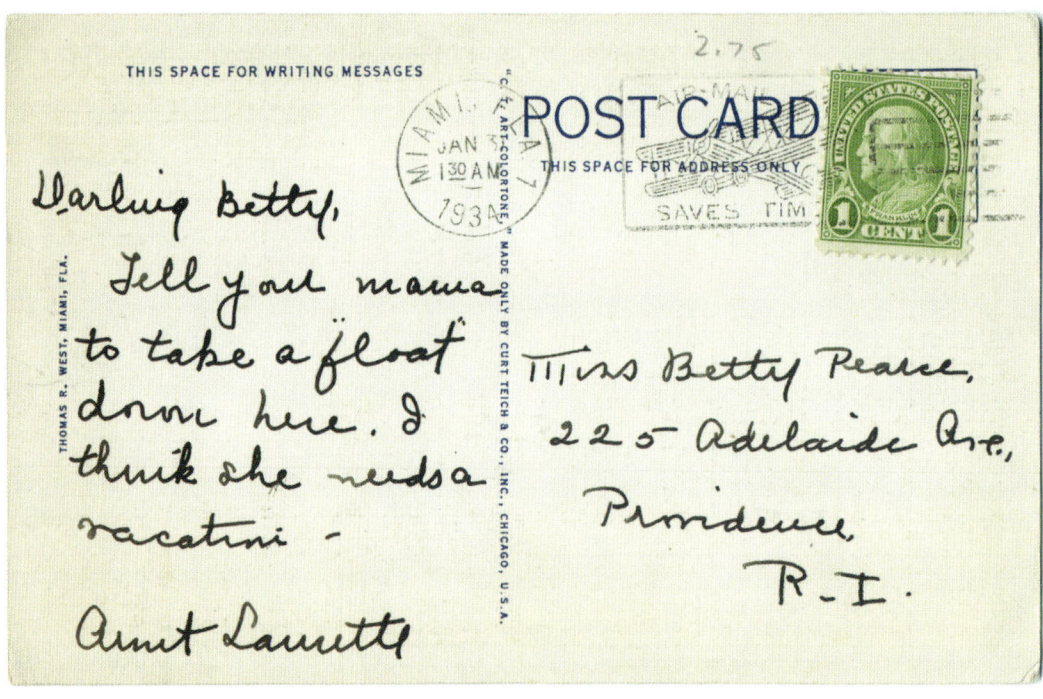

Wars and Warriors

Early nineteenth century events foreshadowed the bloody and tumultuous times that lay ahead for the Seminoles.

From 1813–14 the Creek War took place in Georgia and many of the Upper Creek (known as Red Sticks) survivors fled to Florida to get away from General Andrew Jackson and his forces. Jackson began his rise to fame as an Indian fighter at this time. There were many skirmishes and small battles between the Seminoles, the white settlers and the U.S. military during the early part of the nineteenth century.

The First Seminole War (1816–1818)

The First Seminole War began in 1816 because trade ships at the mouth of the Apalachicola River were being fired upon. General Jackson crossed into Florida and in retribution attacked a poorly armed Negro/Seminole (exiles, as they were called by some) fort near the river. Two stories exist about this raid. One says a lucky shot hit the powder magazine of the fort and blew up the whole place. The other says that an order was given to "give 'em red hot balls," which meant that red hot cannon balls were to be shot into the fort because conventional weapons fire was having little effect. It was said that one of these cannon balls rolled into the powder magazine and the resulting explosion destroyed the fort, killing about 300 people. Despite the fact that the fort was in then-Spanish territory, Jackson felt justified in attacking because he viewed the fort as a threat to trade in the region. It was also considered to be a haven for runaway slaves. Jackson openly advocated taking Florida from Spain anyway.

On November 21, 1817, U.S. Army General Gaines sent Major David Twigs and 250 men to arrest Seminole leader, Neamathla, and they attacked the Seminoles at a place called Fowltown in southern Georgia. Twigs' troops killed and wounded many of them and burned the village. The remaining Indians retreated into the swamps.

General Jackson, whose tremendous ego led him to believe that his word was the law, took command of the situation in 1818 and amassed some 3,500 men near Fort Scott. About 2,000 of these men were Creek warriors who had assembled there with the U.S. Army troops to fight their own kinsmen (warriors from other Tribes, including Shawnees, Saulk, Kickapoos, Choctaws and Delawares, also helped the U.S. forces later in the war). Wholesale destruction of Seminole villages then began and continued for more than two decades.

On September 18, 1823, the Seminoles signed the Treaty of Moultrie Creek, giving up 28,253,820 acres of Florida land in exchange for 4,032,940 acres north of the Peace River in Florida. Also to be provided were $6,000 worth of agricultural equipment and livestock, a $5,000 annuity to continue for twenty years, up to $4,500 for any abandoned improvements, $1,000 per year to maintain a school on the reservation, and $1,000 per year for a blacksmith and a gunsmith. An agreement was made to keep the unauthorized white men off the reservation, and the U.S. was to provide the Indians with meat, salt and corn for one year while they relocated. In effect, the Seminoles were paid about three-fourths of a cent per acre (some say four cents) for the land that they were to leave. This is certainly one of the best examples of how this Tribe of Indians was cheated/forced out of their land. The message given, in a not-so-subtle manner, was — sign or else!

The Florida legislature then passed a law that prohibited the Indians from roaming any land outside the reservation; and, any Indian could be seized if caught doing so. The punishment was a lashing with a whip.

When John Quincy Adams spoke before the United States Supreme Court in 1802, his words reflected the attitude of many American citizens to justify their expansionist views: "What is the Indian title? It is mere occupancy for the purpose of hunting. It is not like our tenures; they (the Seminoles) have no idea of a title to the soil itself. It is overrun by them, rather than inhabited. It is not a true possession."

The whole objective, of course, was to concentrate the Indians in one area and make it easier for their removal at a later date, or so thought the U.S. government.

On May 28, 1830, the U.S. Senate passed the Indian Removal Act and the wheels that drove the chains of horror for all Native Americans were set into motion. A Washington newspaper, the *Niles National Register*, reported that "The miserable creatures will be speedily swept from the face of the earth." Clearly, the personnel at that publication knew nothing about the character or the resolve of the Seminole people. It was an attitude that eventually led to the failure of the United States military to drive them completely from their homeland. To this day, the Seminole Tribe of Florida remains unconquered.

The Seminoles were the last Tribe to feel the effects of the Indian Removal Act of 1830, which was passed after Andrew Jackson became president. They were attacked, coaxed, tricked and hunted. Every attempt was made to remove the Seminoles from their homes and ship them to reservations west of the Mississippi. While some gave up, many did not and were willing to fight to the death to preserve their homeland and their way of life. General Thomas Jesup said, "No Seminole proves false to his country, nor has a single instance ever occurred of a first rate warrior having surrendered."

Famous Seminole leader and medicine man, Sam Jones (Arpeika, Aviaka, Abiaki) was an inspiring leader, hiding out in remote areas of what is now the Big Cypress Reservation and in areas to the west, such as Devil's Garden in the Okaloacoochee Slough, north of what is now Everglades City, Florida. The U.S. military was never able to catch him and, in fact, was never able to get so much as a look at him. Unlike Osceola, Aviaka sometimes chose to remain in the background, leading members of the Tribe to safety in times of great danger. He was also one of the leaders of the Indian forces at the great Battle of Okeechobee.

On December 28, 1835, near present day Bushnell, Florida, the Seminoles attacked Major Francis Dade and his troops.

"Just as day was breaking we moved out of the swamp into the pine barren. I counted, by direction of Jumper, one hundred eighty warriors. Upon approaching the road, each man chose his position on the west side; opposite, on the east side, there was a pond. Every warrior was protected by a tree, or secreted in high palmettos. About nine o'clock in the morning the command approached. In advance, some distance, was an officer on a horse, who, Micanopy said, was a captain; he knew him personally; had been his friend in Tampa. So soon all the soldiers were opposite between us and

the pond, perhaps twenty yards off, Jumper gave a whoop, Micanopy fired the first rifle, the signal agreed upon, when every Indian arose and fired, which laid upon the ground, dead, more than half the white men . . ."

—Alligator (Halpatter Tustenuggee)

The Second Seminole War (1835–1842)

The most violent time in Seminole history — and the longest and most costly Indian conflict ever fought by the United States — was the Second Seminole War. The United States wanted the land that the Indians occupied, and slave owners from the southern part of the country were angered that the Seminoles provided a haven for runaways. So-called interbreeding between the Seminoles and the Blacks was greatly exaggerated, and intentionally so, because the U.S. troops wanted justification for seizing the Blacks, as well as some of the Indians, as runaway slaves.

Seminole warriors named Micanopy, Jumper, and Alligator led a band that ambushed a regiment of soldiers north of Tampa, Florida, on December 28, 1835, and killed 102 of them, including Major Francis Dade, who was shot by Micanopy. The three soldiers who survived later died of their wounds. The Seminoles lost only three warriors and five were wounded. It was a resounding defeat for the U.S. Army and is a battle about which many still marvel to this day. After the Dade Massacre (an action that, if it had been perpetrated by U.S. forces, would likely have been termed a "battle"), the Indians in that vicinity retreated into the Wahoo Swamp — an unmapped, often swampy stretch of land located in what is now Sumter County, Florida; it was heavily wooded in those days and probably was seen as a maze of jungle to the U.S. troops.

The Battle of Withlacoochee, December 31, 1835, was another resounding victory for the Seminoles. Over 700 U.S. troops, including Army regulars and militiamen commanded by General Clinch, attempted to cross the Withlacoochee River by making many trips in an old, leaky, Indian canoe. Eventually, the Army regulars were on one side of the river and the militiamen on the other. Under the leadership of Osceola, 250 Seminoles opened fire on the troops, preventing any further advancement of the U.S. forces. After the hour-and-fifteen-minute battle, the remainder of U.S. troops limped back to Fort Drane. Both General Clinch and Osceola were wounded in the battle.

After the death of Osceola, command of the Seminoles then passed to Coacoochee (Wildcat), and he led them into the fiercest battle of the Seminole Wars on Christmas Day in

Wars and Warriors

1837 near Lake Okeechobee. About 1000–1200 U.S. troops, led by Colonel Zachary Taylor, were at that battle and only 380 Seminoles. (Some authorities on the wars have said that the Seminoles may not have had more than 400 warriors altogether at that period of the war.) The Seminoles positioned themselves in the palmettos, sawgrass (standing five feet high), and in the moss-covered trees, where they even notched the trees to steady their guns. The area was impassable for horses, so any advancement had to be done on foot through about three feet of mud and water. It was an extremely bloody battle and included such famous Seminole War leaders as Billy Bowlegs, Aviaka (Abiaki), Otulke-thloco, and Alligator (this great Tribal leader was only five feet tall). At final count, the Seminoles had 11 dead and 14 wounded; the U.S. Army and an assortment of volunteers from Missouri had 26 dead and 112 wounded. After the Battle of Okeechobee, the Seminoles disappeared into the swamps and the Everglades. This battle, though, was the beginning of the decline of the Seminole's ability to resist the superior numbers of U.S. troops.

Among the Seminoles today, stories are still told of how the sailors and marines would come up the waterways in canoes looking for the Seminoles, jabbing long, sharp sticks into the water in hopes of striking the Indians hiding under water. When one was stabbed, the whole group was discovered. Even children had to be forcibly held under water for the safety of the group, and many drowned. This operation was conducted from 1839 to 1842 by the infamous "Mosquito Fleet" under the command of Navy Lieutenant John T. McLaughlin. Sally Tommie remembers talking with her grandmother, Sally Chupco Tommie, about the days of removal and the horrors they had to endure.

> "They (the U.S. soldiers) would walk along the banks of the waterways where they (the Seminoles) were with a very long stick with a sharp edge poking it into the water . . . She said to me, 'Well, when they're poking the sticks into the water they think we might be hiding underneath there, and if they stab us, they expect us to jump out of the water, and that's when they will find us and anyone else that is hiding with us, so regardless of whether we were pierced while being underneath the water, they would be captured.' So, that's how they were able to escape by maintaining themselves under water . . . that's when they had to take their babies under the water with them, so the babies couldn't cry and they couldn't breathe, and many of them would die."
>
> —as told to Sally Tommie
> by her grandmother, Sally Chupco Tommie

Seminole Views

Wildcat (Coacoochee)

Shown on this card is a famous Seminole leader of warriors during the Second Seminole War. While imprisoned with Osceola at Fort Marion in Charleston, South Carolina, he escaped and became one of the most influential leaders of the Second Seminole War. (Snellings Collection)

Before he was removed to the West, Wildcat replied to Colonel Worth in regard to Seminole removal on July 4, 1841:

"I was once a boy, then I saw the white man afar off. I hunted in the woods, first with bow and arrow, then with a rifle. I saw the white man and was told he was my enemy. I could not shoot him as I would a wolf or a bear; yet like these he came upon me; horses, cattle, and fields he took from me. He said he was my friend; he abused our women and children, and told us to go from the land. Still he gave me his hand in friendship; we took it; whilst taking it, he had a snake in the other, his tongue was forked; he lied, and stung us. I asked but for a small piece of these lands, enough to plant and to live upon far south, a spot where I could place the ashes of my kindred, a spot only sufficient upon which I could lay my wife and child. This was not granted me. I was put in prison; I escaped. I have been again taken; you have brought me back; I am here; I feel the irons in my heart . . ."

After his removal to Oklahoma in 1841, Wildcat decided to go to Mexico where he was granted land by the Mexican president. He made friends with the Kickapoo Indians along the way and the two groups became allies. While there, Wildcat and his band of Seminoles, along with the Kickapoos, helped the Mexican government in their battles against the Mescalero Apaches and Commanches who often made raids into Mexico.

Wars and Warriors

Lake Okeechobee

This tranquil shot on a postcard of "government cut" on Lake Okeechobee gives no indication of the terrible Battle of Okeechobee that took place near the lake. In fact, the scene looked more like the one depicted on the turn-of-the-century postcard shown below. Now threatened by development, the Okeechobee Battleground is in danger of disappearing altogether. The National Trust is leading the way to help preserve this highly significant part of Seminole history. (both from the Snellings Collection)

The Mosquito Fleet had its own problems, though. The terrain was quite hostile with its swarms of mosquitoes, alligators, snakes, sharp-edged sawgrass, and muck (the odor of which was said to have made some of the men quite sick) several feet deep. Traversing such a place was extremely demanding on the sailors and marines, who sometimes had to ford waist-deep water and muck all day in the intense heat, periodically existing on half rations, and at the same time realizing that they were subject to attack at any second. Many of them died, unable to withstand the unrelenting exertion. Their efforts, though only moderately successful, did keep the Seminoles constantly on the run.

Persecution of the Seminoles continued through the rest of Florida until 1842. The cost to the Seminoles was, of course, far greater; they lost many of their Tribesmen, their homes, and their land. According to historical accounts, there were 4,420 (3,824 according to some estimates) Seminoles shipped to the western part of the United States. The personal horrors and generations-old scars of removal cannot be measured.

The Third Seminole War (1856–1858)

In 1854 General Thomas Jesup ordered the construction of large metal boats about 30 feet long and pointed at both ends with a draft of 36 inches or less. They had flat bottoms and were sometimes called alligator boats. These strange vessels were used to patrol the swamps, marshy areas, canals and rivers in search of Seminoles.

First Lieutenant George L. Hartsuff was ordered to monitor Seminole activities, a task which carried him and his troops through the area of Billy Bowlegs' camp. One of the troops stole some bananas from Bowlegs' garden and the following morning Bowlegs led his warriors in a raid and killed the whole group. Thus, the Third Seminole war was underway.

Various raids and skirmishes took place during the following couple of years. Bowlegs, as well as other leaders and warriors, eventually became weary of all the conflicts and did not want them to continue. On March 15, 1858, an agreement was reached with the U.S. government. Afterward, Bowlegs and about seventy-five other Seminoles agreed to leave for the west. At that time a colonel by the name of Loomis, knowing that the remaining Seminoles were few in number and scattered through the swamps, simply declared the armed conflicts to be over and effectively ended the recognized Seminole Wars. The remaining Seminoles now, after so much blood and so many tears, finally got what they had asked for in the beginning — "*Pohaan checkish*" (just leave us alone).

By 1858 the United States had fought three wars with the Seminoles, and the population of the Tribe had been all but eliminated in Florida. Most of them had been removed to the

Wars and Warriors

Seminole Warrior

This postcard depicts a Seminole warrior portrayed in a rather colorful rendition painted by Noah Billie. Warriors wore a long shirt, a neckerchief, a turban (in the folds of which they may have carried a pipe and tobacco), a breechcloth, and occasionally, moccasins. Some wore even less than this. (Snellings Collection.)

West. The 300 or so individuals who remained in Florida, lived in the hammocks (derived from an Arawak word meaning "masses of floating vegetation") of the remotest regions of the swamps and the Everglades, and could never be driven away or enticed in any way to leave their Florida home. It is from this band of hardy men and women that today's Seminole Tribe of Florida developed.

> "Today the newcomers eyes sees that Indigenous Peoples have no more land, they have no more place to live, because the newcomers always create the words to take advantage and take things away which is the property rights, but the eyes of Indigenous People do not see it that way. As long as the wind blows, as long as the sun rises, as long as the blue sky, as long as we see the stars and as long as we walking on the earth, Indigenous People see they still have a home on the earth on this land. When all those things disappear that's the time Indigenous home is taken away and their rights taken away. But all those things are still here and Indigenous People are still here."
>
> —Bobby C. Billie, great, great, great, great, great, great, grandson of Abiaki (Note the spelling of Avaika, and, thus, a different pronunciation, according to Bobby.)

The Seminole Wars cost the United States over $20,000,000 ($7 billion in today's terms). Some estimates were as high as $60,000,000. Forty thousand soldiers and volunteers were deployed during this time. Approximately 1,500 of these men were killed, along with 600 horses, and many more soldiers died of disease. The Seminole conflicts forever changed the conventional tactics of the U.S. military. A few hundred Indians had turned back a large army that was ill equipped to handle what we now call guerilla warfare.

Though the U.S. government is now sorry for the infliction of such tribulation on both the Seminoles and their own soldiers, the war still continues. The weapons now are the words of businessmen and politicians.

The failure of the U.S. military to deal honorably with the Seminoles goes all the way back to the war of 1812. At that time, the Lower Creeks of Georgia, Alabama, and South Carolina were rewarded for their help of the U.S. Army in defeating the Red Sticks (Upper Creeks) by forcing them to cede about eight million acres (approximately two-thirds of their land) to the United States. Many of the Red Sticks fled to Florida and joined the Seminoles. They were not safe from the American military even then because their villages continued to be destroyed as the U.S. Army captured Pensacola and St. Marks from Spain. Ultimately, Spain ceded Florida to the United States. Three years after the Seminole Wars, Florida entered the union.

> "A knowledgeable Indian will often not say too much, and some white folks might mistake us for dumb. But we are taught not to speak too quickly unless we're sure of what we're saying, because words can be like weapons, they can hurt. In our language there is no word for sorry . . . The white man has lots of words for 'I'm sorry.'"
>
> —Sonny Billie

Seminole War Forts

Fort Dallas was the first permanent structure in what is now the city of Miami, Florida. There is some dispute as to the date it was built, but it was in either 1835 or 1839. There is even further dispute as to whose name it bore; some say it was named after Navy Commander Alexander Dallas, while others say it was named after Vice President George Mifflin Dallas who served under President James Polk. In any event, we do know why it was built — because of its easy access to the Everglades to better harass the Seminoles. Military efforts against the Seminoles were also the reasons for building other forts such as Lauderdale, Brooke (the site of which is now beneath the paved streets of downtown Tampa), Drane, Myers, King, Christmas, and others. The location of Fort Dallas at the mouth of the Miami River caused

Fort Dallas

William English purchased the property where Fort Dallas was located from his uncle, Richard Fitzpatrick, two months after the end of U.S. military action against the Seminoles. He constructed houses for 100 slaves and started promoting development and urbanization. The development has been going on ever since. English's land and the fort were reoccupied again in 1849 for fifteen months after the Seminoles killed a government inspector. Finally abandoned in 1858, all but the building pictured in this postcard crumbled to the ground. Over the years the structure has served as a residence, a post office, and even a bar. It was saved from demolition and moved to Lummus Park in 1925. High rise hotels now sit on the original site. (Snellings Collection)

problems from the beginning because of the shallow water around the fort that prevented ships from unloading. For that reason, the fort was abandoned several times.

Many of the campaigns against the Seminoles centered at Fort Dallas. There were ship and boat patrols and riverine expeditions launched down the coast and into the Everglades to locate and destroy the Indians. This combination of forces became a strategy to be used by the United States in later wars. Fort Dallas was turned over to the U.S. Navy in 1842 as the efforts against the Seminoles continued. On May 10, 1842 President John Tyler ordered the end of military efforts against the Seminoles.

Seminoles as U.S. Warriors

The first Seminole to volunteer for modern day military service was Howard Tiger, who served in the U.S. Marine Corps.

Seminoles served in the military as far back as 1862, when 380 men in the First Seminole Cavalry Battalion were scouts in the Confederate Army under the command of Colonel John Jumper and Major George Cloud. In 1864 they raided the Union troops in Indian Territory and along its borders, participating in such actions as the Battle of Cabin Creek. The assembly of these troops was rather amazing because of the fact that the Seminoles had endured hostilities with federal troops and the effects of removal a short time prior to the start of the Civil War.

The Seminole Tribal Color Guard is often present at Native American events, such as the Celebrate Native America Day held each year at Eckerd College in St.

The Seminole Color Guard
Displaying the colors of the State of Florida at "Celebrate Native America Day," March 1999, at Eckerd College in St. Petersburg, Florida. (Snellings Photo)

Wars and Warriors

21

Petersburg, Florida. The Seminole Tribe of Florida Color Guard is well known and respected throughout Indian Country and was featured in the parade of the grand opening of the National Museum of the American Indian in Washington, D.C.

Seminoles who are veterans in today's military are proud of what the United States now represents. The military machine that once persecuted them now welcomes them.

Tribal Chairman Mitchell Cypress

Mitchell Cypress stands for a photo, showing his Tribal Color Guard uniform. The Seminole warriors first started wearing the U.S. Army uniforms that they had taken from downed soldiers. Why they did so is open to speculation, but this practice may have been a symbol of defiance or ridicule of their would-be captors. Now these same uniforms are worn with pride by those Seminoles who serve in the U.S. military. (Courtesy of the *Seminole Tribune*)

Swamp Owl (Virgil P. Morrison, II)

Non-Seminole Re-enactor of Seminole Battles on a Marshtacky Horse

The Marshtacky horse is a short breed that has historically been known for its ability to work well in swampy terrain and for its stamina. These horses served the Tribe well during the nineteenth century, whether working cattle in the thick palmettos or in battle. The warriors who rode these horses were painted with red and black colors and drank water containing snakeroot before battle.

There has never been a non-Seminole to be so consumed by the Seminole culture and history as Swamp Owl. Dressed in full authentic regalia at battle re-enactments, this man presents an image of a nineteenth century Seminole warrior unlikely to be forgotten by any person that sees or hears him.

(Snellings Photo)

Historical Figures

Seminole history is resplendent with colorful characters and strong leaders.

Over the colorful history of Florida's Seminoles are many characters who stand out. Some of these people will be briefly highlighted in this section. As with all cultures, there are people who contribute greatly, those who were in the background and who were the backbone of the Seminoles. The names of some of those are unknown to us now, but their influence will be forever felt by the Tribe.

> "We don't want you to know anything about us. Not even our language, otherwise, you'd know what we're saying."
>
> —Billy Cypress

Josie Billie

Josie Billie

Josie was said to be the first Seminole to wear color stripes on his shirts, which were the forerunners of modern patchwork clothing. (Courtesy of the Fort Lauderdale Historical Society.)

Josie Billie was the son of the notable Billy Conapatchie, who was the first Seminole to attend school. Conapatchie went to school while he was working for Captain F. A. Hendry as a cowboy in Fort Myers. Both Josie and his father were considered by non-Natives to be quite "progressive" for Seminoles at that time. Josie's brother, Billy Fewell (Key West Billy), was also known to like the ways of the white man.

Josie was a well-known medicine man (*ayikomifo:si*) from the area now known as the Big Cypress Reservation. He studied for many years under Tommy Doctor, and he later took over the old man's practice when he died.

In the days before Josie Billie was converted to Christianity, in about 1943, he was often drunk and he became violent and committed various crimes. He is said to have killed two or more Seminoles and had reportedly received a death sentence from the Miccousukee Tribal Council and was ostracized by them in 1937.

He was hunted by the clan of one of his victims. It has been said that Josie went to live on the Big Cypress Reservation at that time. Some of the Miccosukees followed him to the reservation because they did not like the idea of banishing such a powerful medicine man. Thus, there was another early stirring of the Seminole/Miccosukee melting pot.

Josie went on to become a Baptist minister after attending the Florida Baptist Institute in Lakeland, Florida. According to Bobby C. Billie, Josie was 135 years old when he died.

Historical Figures

"So the medicine lives — so the people live."

—*Josie Billie*
(by permission of the Ah-Tah-Thi-Ki Museum)

"James Billie usually makes an example of Josie Billie like the Apostle Paul in the Bible. The Apostle Paul persecuted Christians and things like that and he was changed on the Damascus road. Josie Billie was kind of like that too [i.e. Josie once persecuted Christians who tried to convert Seminoles to Christ]."

—*Cowbone*

"A long way back the Breathmaker blew his breath toward the sky and made the Milky Way. This white way leads to a city in the west where the Big Cypress (*Atsi-na-hufa*) Seminoles go when they die. Bad people stay in the ground right where they are buried. Every time you go through the woods and step where a bad person is buried you feel afraid even though the grave is covered over with bushes and trees. Good people walk over the Milky Way to a city in western sky. Animals take the same path when they die. Long ago animals of an Indian — dogs and horses — were killed so they might go with their masters."

—*Josie Billie* (a pre-Christianity quote)
by permission of the Ah-Tah-Thi-Ki Museum

Naha Tiger

Billy Bowlegs III and Naha Tiger

Together on what may be a hunting party or an afternoon ride near Brighton, Florida. Naha Tiger was an accomplished hunter and cattleman who wore a set of big spurs on his feet — no boots, just spurs. (Snellings Collection)

"... he had about inch thick calluses on his feet. And he would walk right through the sandspurs and anything. And when he did, you know, he was kinda partially blind, you know, he could hardly see too good. But he'd carry binoculars and stand in one spot and look all the way around and see where the cows were and then he'd start walking towards them. They thought he was kinda crazy, you know. I'd say where you been? He'd say I'm gettin' them cows. He had already seen them, you know. He had binoculars though, even out there in the field. They just said yeah — he sells cows — he always gettin' a cow all the time."

—Paul Bowers

Historical Figures

Tom Tiger

Tom Tiger

Tom Tiger (grandfather of Betty Mae Jumper) was not a chief as the caption on this old postcard says; he was a formidable man nevertheless. When his son, Desoto Tiger, was murdered by the famous outlaw, John Ashley, for his pile of animal hides, he lead a party of warriors on an exhausting chase through the Everglades after Ashley. Though hot on his trail, he was unable to catch the man. Ashley was eventually caught and sentenced to hang for that murder, and, after several jailbreaks, he was killed in a shoot-out in 1924. Tom Tiger was killed by a bolt of lightning while building a cypress dugout canoe. (Snellings Collection)

Ingram Billie

Ingram Billie

Famous Seminole medicine man, Ingram Billie (and the grandfather of former Tribal Chairman James Billie), and his family pose for this early postcard. The caption on the card refers to Ruby as a "squaw," a demeaning term sometimes used by non-Indians to refer to Indian women. Some say the names of those shown here with Ingram were Effie Tiger, Jimmie Billie and Johnny Buster, not the ones given on this postcard. (Snellings Collection)

Born in 1890, Ingram Billie (Panther Clan) was the son of Little Billie and Nancy Osceola, who had four sons including Josie Billie, another famous Seminole medicine man. A famous son of Ingram Billie was Frank Billie, who has been called "The George Washington of the Seminole Tribe" because he started the first efforts to organize the Tribe in the '50s.

"He's a grand old man, I'll tell you . . . A lot of things went with him (when he died)."

—Billy Cypress

Historical Figures

The Legend of the Flood

"The earth was once completely covered with water, but before that happened a man made a big boat and a lot of people stayed in it. A fish called a bass dived down and brought up some earth in his mouth. It wasn't much but it was earth from the bottom of the water. A man asked the bass to create some land for the people in the boat, but the bass said 'No, he would not,' and went on to say that he just got that in his mouth (Bass sometimes do that, you know).

"But the man took that ball of mud and made it into a ball and a beaver cut it in two with his tail. Then the man threw one half of the ball of earth toward the south and the other half toward the north. The beaver worked until he made the one to the north into some big countries. The one thrown to the south he made into Cuba.

"The man told everybody in the boat to stay inside four days because it would take that long for the land to dry. After a couple of days the Ivorybill Woodpecker was tired of being in the boat and he got out. The buzzard felt the same way. To this day they stay away from people. The dogs, however, stayed with the people on the boat for four days until the land was dry. Finally, the man let them off the boat. The dogs are still with people."

—*Ingram Billie* (from *Seminole Music,* by permission of the Ah-Tah-Thi-Ki Museum)

Largemouth Bass

A fisherman is landing a nice largemouth bass in this early twentieth century postcard. The largemouth is America's most popular game fish. They have also played a part in the legends of the Seminoles. (Snellings Collection)

Billy Bowlegs

Billy Bowlegs

This postcard of Billy Bowlegs shows how fabulously the man dressed, though he was said to have been short and stocky. This image shows not only his fine coat, but also silver gorgets, silver turban band, rings, fingerwoven diamond-patterned strap, decorative scarves, and what appear to be ostrich or egret plumes. The round piece of metal hanging around his neck is probably the Presidential Medal, given to him by President Millard Filmore in 1852, of which he was quite proud. Though the exact date of the photograph in this postcard is unknown, it is probably one of the earliest photographs of a Seminole Indian. (Snellings Collection)

Billy Bowlegs (Holata Micco) was the major figure during the Third Seminole War. That war started when First Lieutenant George L. Hartsuff raided the garden of Bowlegs and ran off with his prized bananas on December 20, 1855.

Eventually Bowlegs surrendered after relentless efforts of the U.S. troops, who destroyed Bowlegs' personal belongings, dwellings and crops. More Indians were also captured, and Bowlegs finally succumbed to the pressure. He and 75 (some say 165 or 138) of his band boarded the steamship *Grey Cloud* on May 4, 1858, to be shipped west.

During the Civil War, Bowlegs served as a captain in the 1st Regiment of the Indian Home Guard, a Union Army unit in Kansas — a fact the author found quite odd because it had not been very long since he had been removed to the west.

Historical Figures

Billy Bowlegs III

The Family of Billy Bowlegs III

Their pose for this card shows the turban that the men wore and the coin necklaces contrasting against the colorful clothing of these women. This was before the zigzag patterns of today. Billy was an accomplished hunter, guiding such Florida pioneers as the railroad baron, Henry Flagler. (Snellings Collection)

Polly Parker

Polly Parker (Ma-dee-lo-hee)
(Snellings Collection)

Polly Parker (Ma-dee-lo-hee) was captured by the Florida militia during the Third Seminole War near a place called Fisheating Creek, which is near the mouth of the Kissimmee River where it empties into Lake Okeechobee. She was in a group of 39 Cow Creek Seminoles that consisted mostly of women and children. The Cow Creek men were believed to be down in the Everglades with Billy Bowlegs. On May 5, 1858, Polly and the other 38 captives were placed on the Steamer *Grey Cloud* with Billy Bowlegs and his 138 warriors, who, after being paid a substantial amount of money, agreed to emigrate to Arkansas.

The heavily loaded ship had to stop on the St. Marks River for wood to fuel the big boilers. While the wood was being loaded onto the ship, Polly was able to gain permission from the officer in charge to leave the boat with about twelve other Indians to gather some roots and herbs along the edge of the woods for medicine, because some of her people were sick. At an opportune moment when the group was far enough away, using a prearranged signal, all of them scattered into the swamp. Some were recaptured, but Polly was in the group that escaped. Then they gathered together by finding each other using their own owl-like calls.

The group headed southward, but Polly was sick and wanted them to continue without her. They refused and hid her in the swamp, while scouting during the day. At night the others would help her continue on the journey. After eating only berries for three days, they were finally able to spear some garfish and were able to have a meal. They had to be careful with fires to keep from being detected, but now with full stomachs continued on their journey home with renewed spirit.

After many days on the run, Polly and her friends made it back to Lake Okeechobee to their old hunting ground, where they found an old cook pot and a canoe that was hidden in the sawgrass. From there they made their way back to the Everglades to their people. There was a great reunion for Polly with her husband Henry Parker (Hendi-La-Ma-La).

One of Polly's descendants, great grand daughter Sally Tommie, is now the representative of the Fort Pierce group and assistant to Tribal Chairman, Mitchell Cypress. Polly died in 1921 and is said to have lived for over 100 years.

Polly's is just one of the many stories of Seminoles who endured extreme hardship during the days of removal. Egmont Key was the beginning of the Trail of Tears for many members of the Tribe. The ones who had to go there were practically starving when they arrived. They were kept in a stockade like animals waiting for the slaughter. Before they boarded the steamers for New Orleans, several died each day of dysentery and malaria. Many more died en route. In some cases the scene resembled that of the concentration camps during World War II, as many of the captives were forced to lie in their own filth. These things were suffered because of the lust for Florida land and the arrogance of the men who ran the United States during those years. The treatment of Native Americans is one of the saddest and most disgraceful chapters in the history of this nation, of which the Seminole experience is a prime example. Even today there are those who want the Seminole's land and who would like to see the Seminoles relegated to some obscure corners of this nation. More sophisticated means of persecution are in place in modern times, and the Tribe still strives to keep ahead of its enemies.

Joe Dan Osceola

Joe Dan Osceola (Cootihattie is his Seminole name, which means "little frogs got little tails") is one of the friendliest, most colorful and distinguished members of the Tribe. He was the first Seminole to graduate from a public high school — Okeechobee High School in 1957 — where he played quarterback and led their football team to a conference championship in 1955. He eventually went into politics and became the first president of the Tribe.

Joe Dan established the Seminole Tribal Historical Society in 1975, and he was one of the founders of the United Southeastern Tribes, Inc., in 1969. He has also worked with the youth of the Tribe, coaching football and baseball. He now lives on the Hollywood Reservation with his wife, Virginia.

One of the largest Native American gift shops in Florida, The Anhinga, is owned by Joe Dan and Virginia. It is located at the intersection of U.S. Route 441 and Sterling Road in Hollywood near the Seminole Reservation.

Joe Dan Osceola (Cootihattie)

The photo for this card was taken at Okeechobee, where he borrowed the jacket from his cousin so he could pose for the picture. (Snellings Collection)

Historical Figures

"I was elected into the office of the President of the Seminole Tribe from '67 through '71, and at the time there were seven candidates that ran for the office and I won the election. At the time I was only 33 years old, so a lot of the elders thought that I was a little young to be in office. The first year I was in office, the Jaycees selected me as one of 'The Ten Most Outstanding Men in America.'"

—Joe Dan Osceola

"My wife and I have been able to travel the different parts of the United States where the Natives are, and we buy some stuff from them and trade some stuff, my wife makes a lot of Seminole Indian jackets, that's pretty popular, so we trade a lot of stuff for silver and turquoise. We probably have the largest collection of silver and turquoise in the State of Florida."

—Joe Dan Osceola

Micanopy

Micanopy
(Snellings Collection)

Micanopy (Micanopah, Micco Nuppa, which means "topmost king") was a prominent leader in the history of the Seminole Tribe. Not well regarded by some historians, he was said to have been rather stupid and overweight. He weighed 250 pounds and was only 5 feet 6 inches tall. It has been noted that he ate enough breakfast for three people. According to historians, he relied mostly on his subordinates to do the fighting. It has been said that Micanopy had eighty slaves. General Clinch described him as "a man of but little talent or energy of character . . ."

Not all people remember Micanopy in such a manner. Some believe him to have been a strong leader.

"My nation is like a tree of the forest. The branches are children; the leaves, the hair on the head; the sap, the blood; and the bark, the clothing. If you spoil the bark, will it not die? There is nothing to carry the nourishing sap to support the branches, will they not die also? Such then is the case with my people. Take them from their forests and woods, where from childhood they have wandered, will they not pine and die also? If you sow the seeds of disaffection among them, will they not devour each other? If by force you separate them, obliging them to go to the distant land, will they not long to be again with their friends and fathers?"

—*Jumper, brother-in-law of Micanopy, at an 1832 meeting at Payne's Landing*

Historical Figures

Laura Mae Osceola

Laura Mae Osceola (11/13/1932–10/7/2003)

Laura Mae was the first secretary and treasurer of the Seminole Tribe, and she was instrumental in helping to write their constitution, serving as an interpreter for some of the elders. She vehemently opposed those who, at that time, wanted to "phase out" the Seminoles as a recognized Tribe. Laura Mae was also the foster mother of former chairman, James Billie. She married her husband Max (Sr.) back in 1949. They were the first Seminole couple to be married by someone other than a Tribal medicine man. The wedding took place at the First Seminole Baptist Church. Laura Mae believed in practicing and remembering the past while at the same time learning new things to progress in today's world. She taught many of her people to read and write and to embrace education. The result of her efforts helped each person in her life and the Tribe as a whole. A personable lady, she was most kind to the author, and interviewing her was a joy. (Snellings Photo)

Joe Dan Osceola and Betty Mae Jumper Hold the Flag of the Seminole Tribe of Florida

In 1957, seventy-eight years after the U.S. government officially decided that Indians were actually human beings, the Florida Seminoles officially became a recognized Indian Tribe. Betty Mae Jumper and Joe Dan Osceola proudly hold up the flag of their new nation. "In God We Trust" was placed on the official flag. The original founders included such prominent individuals as Max Osceola, Buffalo Tiger, Jimmy Tiger, Billy Osceola, Bill Osceola, Jackie Willie, Laura Mae Osceola, John Henry Gopher, Betty Mae Jumper, Holley Jumper, Frank Billie, Jimmy O'Toole Osceola, Johnny Cypress, and attorney Morton Silver. The first chairman of the Tribe was Bill Osceola. It has now been decided within the Tribe that a person must be at least one-fourth Seminole to become a member of the Tribe. (Snellings Collection)

"We all felt it was important to have the phrase, 'In God we trust.' I feel very strongly about that. Without God, we're nothing. He's responsible for everything."

—Betty Mae Jumper

Historical Figures

The 100th Anniversary of the Dade Massacre

This postcard depicts a meeting of Tribal representatives (left to right) Mike Osceola, an unidentified man, Stanley Hanson, Josie Billie, an unidentified man, Doctor Tiger, Jimmy Billie, Cory Osceola, and then Florida Governor David Sholtz. They were brought to the Tamiami Trail by Stanley Hanson as part of the recognition of the 100th anniversary of the Dade Massacre. The meeting took place near the Tamiami Trail on February 22, 1936. All the Seminoles asked for in this meeting was to be left alone. (Snellings Collection)

Independent Traditional Seminoles have never accepted membership in the Seminole Tribe of Florida. They don't believe that they need to be recognized by the U.S. government and they do not want any part of life on a reservation.

"Reservations take away the ability to work with the earth. Once you destroy that, all things will be gone."

—Bobby C. Billie

Seminole Views

Buffalo Tiger

Buffalo Tiger
(Snellings Photo)

Buffalo Tiger became chief of the Miccosukee Tribe for 33 years, and eventually led them to national recognition in 1961. (Those Indians who speak the Miccosukee [Hitchiti] language have also been referred to as I.laponki). He is an expert in Indian crafts and still has many handmade items for sale in his store at Buffalo Tiger's Florida Everglades Airboat Rides forty miles west of Miami on U.S. Route 41. The airboat tour phase of his business prospers as countless tourists ride his airboats into the Everglades. He laments the old 'glades, though, reliving the days of yesteryear in conversations with those who inquire. He talked of once crystal clear water, blue sky, no pollution, and a seemingly endless supply of wildlife: "I saw all these things . . . it all dances together, and then one day I looked up and they were gone."

Buffalo saw the onslaught of white people in the early part of the twentieth century, as the Everglades was drained, facilitating the ever-increasing hoard of tourists and overdevelopment intruding from the east coast. He was in his teens before he played with white children, yet he remembers lying in the grass watching them. As time went on, the Everglades National Park was established and the Miccosukees were removed from over two million acres of land they called home. He and other Indians realized that they had to adapt to the white man's world to survive.

In addition to helping to establish the Seminole Tribe of Florida, Buffalo Tiger was also instrumental in establishing the Miccosukee Tribe of Indians of Florida. A lot of frustrating meetings were held with U.S. government officials, and the Miccosukees were about to be written out of existence by the U.S. The founders of the new Tribe threatened to get the help of Fidel Castro, going so far as to make a trip to Cuba. The Miccosukees had already been

Buffalo Tiger and Friends

Buffalo Tiger (right rear), Josie, Tommy, and Bobby Tiger and their friends Mike, Homer, Douglas, Howard, and John Osceola enjoyed playing around a big stuffed gator at Musa Isle that was often used as a photo prop in those days. (Snellings Collecton)

recognized by six other nations and Cuba was to be the seventh. If that had been finalized, the Miccosukee Tribe of Indians of Florida would have been recognized by the United Nations as a sovereign nation. Not wanting that to happen, the U.S. Government finally recognized the Tribe on January 11, 1962. Some Seminoles say that the main reason the Miccosukees split from the Seminole Tribe was the fact that they were unable to get any of their people elected to positions of leadership, being always outvoted by the Indians at Brighton and Hollywood, Florida.

The Miccosukees have always prided themselves in maintaining the "old ways." In the mid-twentieth century some Seminoles wanted to receive federal aid and adopt some of the white man's ways while still maintaining their Indian identity. The more traditional members of the Tribe did not want financial or any other kind of governmental assistance; they simply wanted to be left alone. All they wanted was land where they could live and pursue their interests.

There is yet another group of Seminoles that disavows both the Seminole and Miccosukee Tribes. They are called the traditionalists, the Independent Traditional Seminole Nation.

Seminole Views

"I live in a village 38 miles southeast of Naples, Florida. I am spokesman for my village of 12 people. I hold no land deed by the white man's standard. I hold only my Indian title and right of occupancy to this land. My family and I live where we choose, as we always have. There are some Indian people who have turned their backs on their own people, their traditions, and way of life. These people speak for a small handful of people only. Our tradition is, by not being present at meetings, means a vote of no. There were many more Indian people not at the January meeting than there were people there who voted. I do not live on a reservation, and I was not informed of this meeting. If I had been, I and my people would not have voted for selling of our land. Our God gave us this land for us to live on, hunt, fish, and live in peace. Every year the white man tries to take more and more of our Indian land from us. He does not try to know and respect our ways of life. He tries to make us one of his. We are different from the white man, with different beliefs and customs by which we live. The selling of our land is against the way of life and custom of any true traditional Seminole Indian. We have always been in this land. We have always been able to hunt, fish, to cut wood for our homes, and live where we wished. We do not wish to give up our rightful claim to our land."

—*Guy Osceola*

Historical Figures

Bobby C. Billie

Bobby C. Billie

Spiritual leader of the Independent Traditional Seminole Nation of Florida. He does not necessarily endorse all of the information contained in this book. (Snellings photo)

"You (European man) came in here to not understand how we live and how we respect life and you miss manage us and you abuse us, so let's not do that again, not the way the Creator want us to be with the earth. That's what I tell people because we been talking about the battle and how you did all those things to us . . . Only the Creator said you always forgive me, you have to have forgiveness, love and care for all things. That's our road for life. They (the elders) said no matter what your enemies have done to you, you turn around and lend a hand. We all need to do this."

—Bobby C. Billie

Billy Osceola

Billy Osceola

Shown here with a bow and arrows, Billy Osceola was said to be a very kind and gentle man, and he was once chairman of the Tribe. Most Seminoles today are that way, yet they remain skeptical of the outsiders and are secretive about much of their culture.

Bows and arrows similar to the ones shown in this postcard are seldom used now, but the young men of the Tribe were known to be quite proficient with these weapons during the eighteenth and nineteenth centuries (and probably for eons before), as they hunted small game and birds. According to the Ah-Tah-Thi-Ki Museum staff, Seminole bow and arrow shafts are made from the stems of the myrsine plant (Snellings Collection)

Historical Figures

Annie Tommie

Annie Tommie at the Pirate's Cove Camp in Miami

Annie Tommie was one of the most famous matriarchs of the Seminole Tribe. She was born in the Everglades in 1856 during the Third Seminole War. She had little contact with settlers during the early part of her life and grew up mostly in isolation from them. By the turn of the century she achieved a significant position of authority as a medicine woman.

Annie helped bridge the gap between the old days of living in isolation to the modern era of reservations. Her camp was the last one in the city of Fort Lauderdale. She and her family were the first Seminoles to settle on the reservation established by the federal government west of Dania, Florida. There she remained a very influential matriarch until her death in 1946. (Snellings Collection)

Seminole Views

Tony Tommie

Annie Tommie and her son, Tony Tommie

Annie Tommie's son, Tony Tommie, was the first Seminole to attend public school in the Fort Lauderdale, Florida, public school in 1914. This opportunity was provided through the efforts of Mr. Lucien A. Spencer and Mrs. Frank Stranahan. Tony did well in school and later brought some of his friends, as well. (Snellings Collection)

Tony Tommie assumed leadership of the Fort Lauderdale Band of Seminoles at the age of 19; however, in 1926 Tony came into disfavor among the Seminoles because he falsely represented himself as chief and wrote to President Calvin Coolidge, stating that the Seminoles were ready to become U.S. citizens. Tony also got some Tribal members involved in a publicity stunt, involving the sale of some 150,000 acres of drained Everglades land, for which the theme was "The Seminole Indians, Ancient Masters of the Everglades, Surrender The Sovereignty of the Muck Lands To Their Paleface Brothers." Upon hearing of this deed, the Tribal council was furious, and the powerful Tribal leaders, Josie and Ingram Billie, had attorney and friend W. Stanley Hanson draft a letter to Senator Duncan Udall Fletcher, disclaiming the authority and assertions of Tony Tommie.

Historical Figures

Annie Jimmie

Annie never learned English and she always dressed in traditional clothes. Born on January 1, 1903, she remembered the old stories that her elders told, and they warned her that the earth is getting old . . . that houses would pop up everywhere — even in the Everglades. The crops and fruits and vegetables would not be good. At her death on July 24, 2003, she believed that was where we were headed.

"Our matriarchal society is a society that respects and reveres the women of the Tribe. The women in the Tribe are the main one's that are able to keep the Tribe going by giving birth and nurturing their children. When a mother is of one clan, her child is automatically of that clan, so not only does she keep her Tribe blossoming, she continues that clan as well, so her roll in the Seminole Tribe, as far as I know and the one I can speak on personally, is highly respected and should be in every race of people; but I know here is the way it is."

—Sally Tommie

Annie Jimmie at Home
(Snellings Photo)

Cory Osceola

Cory Osceola, Tihokee Osceola and Henry Cypress

Pictured here in a photo-postcard made about 1906. Cory and Henry became influential leaders of the Tribe years later. (Snellings Collection)

Cory Osceola

(Snellings Collection)

Cory Osceola was one of the most prominent leaders of the Seminoles during the twentieth century. Cory was "headman" at Musa Isle, where he took care of the salaries for the Tribal members who worked there and organized the trips they took. He was literate (which is more than can be said for many white men of his day), and he managed the gift shop at Musa Isle. While working in the fields he became foreman and hired many of the hands to do the planting and picking of the crops. He eventually operated his own tourist attraction on the Tamiami Trail near Naples, Florida, until his death in 1978.

Historical Figures

49

Cory Osceola and Family

Cory Osceola, his wife Juanita and daughter, Tahama (the first Seminole to be born in a white man's hospital), pose for a photo at Musa Isle. Cory and Juanita were married at Musa Isle, breaking the tradition of a marriage at the Green Corn Dance. The event was seriously scorned by Tribal elders of that day. It has been said that Cory and his new wife received death threats because of what they did. Cory was really a medicine man, but white men labeled him chief. Medicine men were actually the leaders of the Tribe. Today's number one Seminole leader is still called chief by non-Indians, but his real title is chairman. (Snellings Collection)

Osceola

Osceola (1804–1838)

Billy Powell was his English name. He was also known as Tallahassee Tustenuggee and Asanyole. (Snellings Collection)

Osceola, according to some historians, was "a little below common height," with small hands and feet, piercing eyes and chiseled lips. He often had a continuous smile on his face when dealing with officers of the military, and he greeted them with a firm handshake. The name Osceola is believed by some to be a white man's corruption of the name Asiyaholo, which means "black drink singer." This name indicates that this person was one of the sons of the man who offered the black drink to participants in the Green Corn Dance. He was said to have been quite proficient at drinking the brew, hence the name. Osceola was also called Powell, which was the name of his Scottish father. Osceola was born on the Tallapoosa River in Georgia. His mother is believed to be of mixed Indian ancestry.

While Osceola was trading at Fort King, his wife, Chechoter (Morning Dew), was captured by some white men to be their slave because she was part Black and thought to be a fugitive slave. Osceola was placed in irons when he understandably became full of rage. Osceola never forgave what he considered an insult, not only to him, but to all Seminoles. This incident was one of the main causes of his tremendous hostility toward the whites and was said by some to be the cause of the start of the Second Seminole War.

On December 18, 1835, Osceola led a raid on a supply train near Payne's Prairie, and ten days later the famous attack on Major Francis L. Dade took place near what is today the town of Bushnell, Florida. At that time Osceola was filled with remaining bitterness at the capture of his wife, and he made a point to kill Indian Agent Thompson, the man with whom

Historical Figures

he was doing business when she was captured, and Thompson's dinner companion, Lieutenant Smith.

At a December 28, 1835, meeting of other Indian leaders with Indian Agent Wiley Thompson — whom he later shot — Osceola said:

"My brothers! The white people got some of our chiefs to sign a paper to give our lands to them, but our chiefs did not do as we told them to do; they done wrong; we must do right. The agent tells us we must go away from the lands we live on — our homes, and the graves of our fathers, and go over the big river among the bad Indians. When the agent tells me to go from my home, I hate him, because I love my home, and will not go from it."

Osceola

This postcard depicts the famous portrait of Osceola by George Catlin in 1837. (Snellings Collection)

Another quote from that meeting with Indian Agent Wiley Thompson at Fort King in April of 1835 was a little more forceful and has been remembered through the ages as the trademark of Osceola. Breaking through the group (which included, among others, Sam Jones, Alligator, Jumper, and Micanopy), Osceola shouted, as he drove his hunting knife through the treaty that put forth conditions of Seminole removal to the west, "The only treaty I will ever make is this!" He hurled his knife into the table that separated him from the Americans. "I will make the white man red with

Osceola, continued

blood. I will blacken him in the sun and the rain, where the wolf shall smell of his bones and the buzzard live upon his flesh." (Some historians say that it is quite possible that a certain amount of "poetic license" was taken in the recording of Osceola's words.) John K. Mahon, author of *History of the Second Seminole War*, describes Osceola in a letter to the author:

"Osceola rose suddenly into leadership in 1834, when he forcefully told the United States officials that the Seminoles would never leave Florida. For the next year and a half his nerve, activity and intelligence diffused through the Seminole groups and stiffened them against the encroachments of white people. He had no clan, Tribal bloodline to give him leadership status. He was, in fact, a half-breed. Powered by his determination not to be driven out of the homeland, he made the role as leader himself. He was instrumental in bringing the Seminoles up to a fighting pitch. One U.S. soldier was said to have remarked, '. . . I tell you, he was a great man; education would have made him the equal of Napoleon.'

"From late in 1835 to the summer of 1836, if it can be said that the Seminoles had a general, he was it. Well into the summer of 1836, the Indians were winning the conflict. But beginning in that summer illness sapped his vitality and his followers dropped away. He apparently used the last of his energy as a leader on the night of June 2, 1837, when he and Sam Jones spirited away several hundred Seminole prisoners awaiting deportation at Fort Brooke. Several weeks later, by General Thomas S. Jesup's order, he was captured under the flag of truce.

"Several other Indian leaders in the Second Seminole War deserve at least equal credit with Osceola for the gallantry of their fight to stay in their homeland. Conspicuous among them were Coacoochee (Wildcat) and Arpeika (Sam Jones [also known as Abiaka or Abiaki]), but now myth enveloped them. Osceola will always loom larger than life size in the story of the Seminole Indians."

Historical Figures

Captured at Fort Peyton, by the U.S. Army on October 27, 1837, he died of malaria in January of 1838 at this fort where he was imprisoned after being removed to Charleston, South Carolina, from St. Augustine, Florida. The inscription marking the grave of Osceola reads as follows:

Osceola — the Rising Sun, may the Great Spirit avenge you, keep you, love you and cherish you, — the Defender of your country.

Osceola's Grave at Fort Moultrie in Charleston, South Carolina

As a tribute to this gallant man, Osceola's name is borne today by twenty towns, three counties, two townships, one borough, two lakes, a state park, and a national forest. Few men have such a legacy (Snellings Collection)

Seminole Views

Interesting Reverse Sides of Seminole Cards from the Snellings Collection.

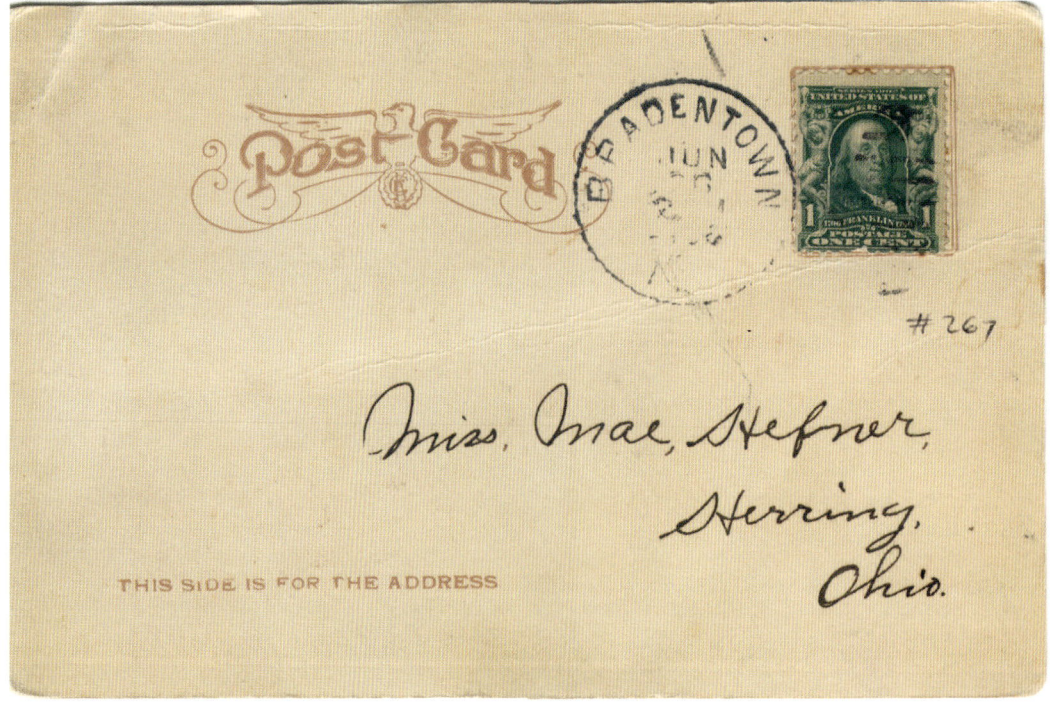

4

Black Seminoles

Black Seminoles have played an important role in the history of the Seminole Tribe.

Plantation owners from Georgia and the Carolinas were quite upset that the Seminoles provided escaped Black slaves a safe haven. They were so upset about it that they made raids across the Florida border to try to capture them, which was one of the main factors that began the Seminole Wars. It was estimated that there were about 1,400 Blacks living among the Seminoles in 1836.

John Cavillo, known to the Seminoles as "Gopher John" because he liked to eat gopher tortoise, was a tall athletic man, known for his courage and marksmanship. He was sometimes referred to as John "Horse." John was a popular guide, cook and interpreter. Like many other Black Seminoles, he was known to be a fierce warrior and helped the Seminole leader, Wildcat.

A man named Abraham was one of the most influential Black Seminoles. He was an advisor and interpreter for Chief Micanopy. He was also called "The Prophet" because he was known to be deeply religious, even though he was accused of drunkenness and

Black Seminoles

The two people in this postcard are probably descendents from slaves who escaped before the Civil War and fled to the then-Spanish territory of Florida. Common for that day, the man in this postcard is sporting an egret plume on his hat. (Snellings Collection)

deceit. He was nevertheless a very intelligent man and even accompanied Micanopy and a delegation of Seminoles to Washington, DC.

Yet another Black Seminole called Louis was fluent in four languages and noted for his ability as a guide. Under the guise of leading the U.S. troops under the command of Major Francis Dade to Fort King, he instead led them into position in the Great Wahoo Swamp, where the Seminoles attacked and wiped out the whole unit except for one man.

Though Seminoles were known to have Black slaves, they were considered friends and allies and were treated with respect. Of course, they had in common that they were both persecuted by the white man.

Some Black Seminoles, however, were not always loyal to their Indian friends. The U.S. military used some of these Blacks to guide them to Seminole encampments. Some of these Blacks saw "the handwriting on the wall" and decided that the Indian position was not a good one. In such cases, loyalty to the Red Man's cause began to wane.

"A lot of them intermarried with the Seminoles, and as a matter of fact, during the Indian wars they became interpreters for the Seminoles, because they learned how to speak the Seminole language and, of course, the white man's language by working on a plantation somewhere, and then when they finally escaped, they came down to Florida to live among the Seminoles."

—*Joe Dan Osceola*

Black Seminoles

"The old Seminole chief, Miami, Fla.," the card reads. Well, this elderly man, who appears to be a Black or Cow Creek Seminole, was not a Seminole chief, and the photo was likely not taken in Miami. Chipco, a warrior during the Second Seminole War, and his nephew are said to have settled near Catfish Lake, which is known today as Lake Pierce, near the famous Bok Tower in Lake Wales, Florida. The people of this group were known to wear kerchiefs around their heads in the manner depicted in this postcard. Tallahassee eventually assumed leadership of this group and became quite friendly with the whites of that area. This band of Seminoles moved to Fisheating Creek on the north side of Lake Okeechobee and, after uniting with other camps, formed the Cow Creek Seminoles. Many of the Seminoles on the Brighton Reservation are descendants of this group.

The Old Seminole "Chief"
(Snellings Collection)

Publishers of these postcards often put arbitrary labels or names on them for marketing purposes, with little or no thought about the people depicted in the cards. Sometimes, even books about Seminoles were published with countless errors; the authors became self-appointed experts on the Tribe.

"White man writes what he wants to write, he never asks a question, he just assumes because he thinks he's superior."

—James Billie

The Family of Mrs. Charlie Willie

During a short period of time in Seminole history, shortly after the turn of the century, black top conductor's hats and bowlers were popular items of clothing for the men. The men are also sporting new pants, vests, watch chains, and ties. This postcard was made prior to 1907. (Snellings Collection)

Housing

The Seminoles transitioned from log cabins to chickees when the U.S. government arrived.

The open-sided, thatched huts pictured in the postcards on the following page are called *chickees* (*chigets*, by some Seminoles). The Mikasuki word for them is *ciki*, meaning "house." Some say that these thatched houses originated with the Calusas, an early indigenous tribe in Florida.

Chickees have a platform that is raised about three feet off the ground and covers the whole inside of the structure. This platform provides protection from floodwater and various creatures, such as snakes. The platform also provides an area for bedding and keeps other important items away from moisture. Below the platform is a good area in which to temporarily store items, such as tools; it's also a great place for the old family dog to lie. The platform is supported by beams that run the entire length of the chickee. These beams are split logs with the flat side turned up and tied to the structural supports with rope.

The roof of the chickee is thatched with palmetto fronds; it is about 12 feet high in the center. The main supports for the structure are eight cypress logs. Logs are also bound together and placed on top of the roof with several logs on each side of the ridge to keep it in place. There are no rooms in a chickee, but a cloth is often used to pull down for privacy or for protection from mosquitoes (*hos-ko-ton-I*). Surprisingly strong, the *chickees* withstand bad storms and provide shelter from the hot sun and the frequent rains during the summer months.

There are separate purposes for different chickees: one is for cooking (usually in the center of the camp), one is for sleeping, one is for storage, etc. Women often sewed their clothing using hand-cranked Singer sewing machines on a platform in one of the chickees.

Seminoles didn't always live in these thatched huts. This practice came about during the nineteenth century, when they became fugitives who were more mindful of avoiding the U.S. Government, which was trying to rob them of their land and remove them from their Florida homes. When necessary, the Seminoles could leave these simple dwellings at short notice and move to another location.

"It was told to me from the beginning when the white people got here, the Seminoles and the Miccosukee lived in log cabins. The Seminoles are not from this area, which you see as Hollywood now, but again, it could be because the Seminoles consist of sixteen different small bands, or different tribes in the state of Florida and finally became organized as one unit in 1975. Around Gainesville and that area, they lived in log cabins. During the Indian removal, like when they started fighting with soldiers, they would stay there like a month or a year or two until they see their enemy coming, and they would move on, and that was the quickest way to keep shelter for the families in the tribe during the war. Then after that, modern time was very advantageous for the Seminole and Miccosukee, the way to make a living, the people who owned hotels and bars all the way to Key West, whichever direction you want to go, like towards Jacksonville or Pensacola, they have big, big huts. Natives, Seminole and Miccousukee, can make their living off of that full time if they want to work at it (building chickees), but it's not an easy job like the summer they have to work pretty hard, under the hot summer sun in order to finish the huts. Seminoles lived in them (chickees) a long time like this during the war and after the war as well. But before the war they used to live in log cabins."

—*Joe Dan Osceola*

Housing

61

Chickees Near the Turn of the Twentieth Century

(Snellings Collection)

Annie Tommie and Seminole Children in Front of a Chickee

Annie Tommie gathers children about her for the picture taken for these early postcards. It was often the custom in the early twentieth century to pose for these types of photos and for tourists who wanted to take some pictures.

(Snellings Collection)

In 1934 the Indian Reorganization Act was passed by Congress, which provided for reservation expansion; men like John Collier and James Glenn made every possible effort to help the Seminoles. Sometimes they even worked with little or no pay. Federal officials came to the earthshaking conclusion that the traditional Seminole way of life should be encouraged.

Five reservations exist today: Brighton (named after James B. Bright, who built a hotel in 1924 that featured many Seminole crafts), Tampa, Big Cypress, Immokalee, and Dania (Hollywood), where the Tribal headquarters is now located. A new reservation is proposed for the Cow Creek Seminoles near Fort Pierce. The Miccossukee Reservation is located on U.S. Route 41 (Tamiami Trail).

The Tamiami Trail did much to facilitate trade (especially the tourist trade) and to open up the Everglades to development. The $13 million project changed the area forever and the chiseling-away at this unique wilderness began in earnest after its completion.

Chickees in a Temporary Camp Near Miami

In the 1920s temporary camps like this one sprang up along the Tamiami Trail (Hwy. 41) as the Indians did their trading near Miami. *(Snellings Collection)*

Housing

63

Clan Members Pose at Chestnut Billie's Camp

Mona Tiger Billie (far left), Charlie Billien, Jack Motlow, and Jane Tiger pose with their clan members for a postcard photo at Chestnut Billie's Camp. Chestnut Billie's Camp was one of the main villages during the early part of the twentieth century. Such camps were commonplace during that era, and they were usually built on high ground so they would not be flooded during the rainy season and where gardens would be more likely to flourish. *(Snellings Collection)*

Seminole Views

Typical Chickee and Camp Construction

This card was printed in both a colorized version and in black and white. It shows a Seminole village, probably in the Everglades, around the turn of the twentieth century. The scene shows typical chickee and camp construction of that period. *(Snellings Collection)*

Traditional Food

Seminoles still enjoy traditional dishes,
such as hearts of palm, turtle soup and sofkee.

Some traditional Seminole food and yesteryear's village kitchens are totally unfamiliar to most of the outside world. Their diet today is much like the white man's, but they still enjoy traditional dishes such as wild game, garfish, roasted corn, heart of the cabbage palm, turtle soup, and sofkee (sofkie).

The traditional Seminole beverage known as sofkee (derived from the Muskogee word for corn syrup) was made by women who ground corn with a mortise (*kitchit*) and pestle (*kishtubit*) to make the necessary bread ingredient. This corn flour was sifted through palmetto fibers and placed in a kettle of boiling water. (The drink was also made from commercial grits purchased from a trader's store.) Venison, frog's legs, pork or alligator meat was then added to the mixture.

Flour was also hand ground from the roots of the zamia and/or the similax plants. Some authorities think that this use of the zamia plant indicates that there was contact with people in the West Indies, since similar techniques were practiced there. After pounding the roots, the women strained, dried and baked the pulp to make bread.

Seminole Views

Making Sofkee

Louise Billie and Mary Billie Larkin pound corn to be used to make sofkee, a Seminole drink. Notice the capes that they have around their shoulders; they were not only used for decorative clothing, but also shielded them from mosquitos. (Snellings Collection)

"SOFKEE is something I grew up drinking. When I drink sofkee now it helps me to reminisce of a different time and era in my life. It brings back a point in time when I was young and enjoying myself and memories of my grandmother. I don't drink sofkee very much now. Back then it was always around. It was either on a stove or hanging out over the fire outside — grits or corn or rice sofkee. I distinctly remember smelling the real putrid smell of that coontie plant as they processed it. And I mean it smelled bad. I remember my grandmother had those four poles under the sheet tied to them. She'd go out and get that root from the plant, she'd soak it and the juice would dry out and then she would get the dried root and chop it and make it into a brew that really tasted good."

—Moses Jumper, Jr., from Echoes In the Wind

"Seminoles made flour from the coontie plant, which is poisonous. You dig up the roots and make them into a pulp using a homemade grater. The poison is washed out by using a strainer. You dry what's left over and that becomes flour for making bread."

—by permission of the Ah-Tah-Thi-Ki Museum

Traditional Food

"Cooking Chickee"

This is a postcard of a painting by famed Seminole artist, Noah Billie. (Snellings Collection)

"Women are not supposed to stand up and eat. And you're not supposed to lay down and eat. . . . If you lay down and eat, if you're a woman, then someone will take your husband away from you. And then if you're a woman and you stand up and eat, woman's sickness, you will have it."

—Lottie Shore

Seminole Views

A rule of thumb for the Seminoles is to eat when you're hungry, not on a set schedule of three meals per day. In the old days a pot of stew was kept on the fire in the village for Indians to come eat whenever they wanted to eat. A special chickee was built for cooking where pots and pans were suspended from the ceiling and other supplies kept on the floor.

Another Tribal custom was that members of each Clan must eat with other members of that same Clan; for example, a member of the Wind Clan cannot eat with a member of the Otter Clan. This is another practice not strictly observed today.

The Cooking Fire

Ada Tiger, Agness Jumper, James Jumper and Cordell Jumper sit before the cooking fire. All of the family, including children, had their chores to do, whether it was carrying water, helping with the meals, or just running errands. (Snellings Collection)

"Deer meat, turtle soup, fry bread and sofkee were things that still give me a warm fuzzy feeling that depicted 'home.' I, as did all of us, had daily chores to do — and we all did them — because we were expected to. There was always an uncle around that would make sure we toed the line. If we didn't, there were always needles for scratching, and we knew our disobedience and poor attitudes were sure to be dealt with."

—Virginia Mitchell

Traditional Food

The traditional Seminole foods were totally unfamiliar to the new assistant to Chairman James Billie in 1979. Not everyone knows what a "gopher" is, especially some of the new employees back in the 1970s. Pat Diamond, the former secretary to the chairman, related this humorous tale:

I'm from West Virginia and from a rural background and a different type of culture than from around here. I'm from the Appalachian Mountains, hunting squirrels and this type of thing. I'd been here about three weeks, when the health director and the assistant health director, who were Cecil Johnson and Joel Frank, came to me and they said, "We're going to go to Immokalee next week, and you're going to go with us."

I said, "Oh, okay." Well, first of all, I didn't know where Immokalee was; I'd never heard of Immokalee.

They said don't worry about taking lunch 'cause they're going to cook for us.

I said, "Oh, okay."

So the day before we get to Immokalee, Cecil looks at me and said, "Did you ever eat gopher?"

I said, "No, I've had squirrel and rabbit." I thought, "Gopher is going to be in that family." So I thought, "Oh, gosh, what am I going to do?" At that point in my life I was a picky eater, and I thought, "I'm never going to get this past my mouth, we're going to have a real problem here."

Pat Diamond,
Former Secretary to the Chairman
(Courtesy of Pat Diamond)

He was explaining that it was a Seminole delicacy. I had not been exposed to at all to the real camp cultural thing, I had only been exposed to the business office, this was going to be my first field trip.

First we get to Immokalee, and at the time they were still living in the chickees. It was a very rural reservation, a piece of land, I don't even know if it was a Federal Reservation at the time. When you pulled up they were still in their chickees, the women cooked in the community fire, they had all the women out there over the open fire in their beads and skirts. First of all I thought I was going to have a heart attack. I felt like I had driven into a *National Geographic* magazine. The way it was located, it was far enough off the road that you were in another world. I'm in awe to start with, I'm just a little dumb hillbilly. And to see them cooking and all this.

In my mind I'm wondering, "How am I going to handle this gopher?" I thought, "I can't hurt their feelings, I can't do anything to embarrass them, I can't embarrass myself, and I'm on a ninety-day probation and I'm not going to make it past this, this is it."

It comes time to eat, I'm the only non-Indian there.

So Cecil turns around and looks at me and says, "We're ready to eat now, you can go first."

"Why do I have to go first?"

"Because you're the guest."

"Why am I the guest?"

"Well, because you're the non-Indian."

I'm now starting to break out in a sweat, because I know I really got a problem here, and I don't know how I'm going to handle it, so we go around the end of this table. After having seen these older women looking like Suzie (reference made to the late Suzie Jim Billie of Big Cypress) out there cooking in their beads, skirts and all that, I was expecting the gopher.

So we go around the corner, well here they got meatloaf, they got bread still in the bag, they had fry bread, they had potato salad, they had beans and something else. I thought I had been saved 'cause they had meatloaf, now I'm thinking, "I'm going to live through this, I'm going to make it."

After we finish eating, Cecil turns around and looks at me and asks me what did I think of the gopher?

I said, "I didn't eat any gopher."

He said how did I know?

"Because I'm from West Virginia and we had squirrel and we had rabbit and there was no gopher there."

He looked at me and started dying laughing. He said, "You're talking about a prairie gopher."

I said, "Yeah, what else is there?"

Traditional Food

He said, "I'm talking about gopher turtle."

I thought, "Oh, my God, I might have eaten one."

By the time I left there I realized there had been no turtle served. It was one of the nicest days except for the beads of sweat on my forehead. It was the most traumatic, I felt like, once I made it past that gopher turtle deal, I felt like I could handle anything else in this organization. Twenty years later I still haven't eaten any gopher.

—*Pat Diamond*

Gopher Tortoise

This old postcard shows a gopher tortoise, which was a delicacy among the Seminole Tribe before it became threatened in much of his habitat. (Snellings Collection)

Seminole Views

Sugarcane

This postcard was made almost a century ago, when sugarcane was harvested by hand and we were a far cry from the giant industry of today. (Snellings Collection)

"Some people used it in their coffee for sweetener, and with their potatoes, the wild potatoes . . . They made candy out of it, they reboiled it until it got hard."

—*Alice Snow*
(by permission of the Ah-Tah-Thi-Ki Museum)

Seminole Kitchen at Musa Isle

Mickey Tiger is skinning a garfish as she prepares it for the fire. Sallie Tiger and Annie Jim wait behind her. (Snellings Collection)

Traditional Food

A Manatee

Manatees like the one shown in this old postcard were hunted for food by the Seminoles during the early nineteenth century. The Indians not only used the animals themselves, they sold manatee meat to the British turtle hunters who came to the Florida Keys. The Seminoles harpooned manatees from a canoe, using a harpoon that had a buoy attached to it so the animals could be located when they sank. They simply waited for the manatee to surface for air and shot it. The meat is said to have a taste similar to pork. Today the manatee population has greatly declined as a result of injuries inflicted by boat propellers. Manatees are now protected by law. (Snellings Collection)

Cooking Pots

This early photo postcard shows cooking pots hanging at Chestnut Billie's Camp. Pots were hung in this manner in the camps around the turn of the twentieth century. While there was some problem with sanitation, most of the Tribe remained healthy. This card is one of the many that were published by R. R. Doubleday of Council Bluffs, Iowa, in the early part of the twentieth century. Postcards such as this one are valuable photographic records of the Seminoles of that day. (Snellings Collection)

"Mealtime they got platform, big platform, and when they cook the food, meal, drink, make rice or gravy, they just put it on the table. The men eat first and the women eat what was left. That's the way when they cook it, they put it on big platform and put it in the middle and fathers and children and men sit around and eat, and after that they put some more in there and when the men get out the women sit there and eat. . . . In my day, you know we don't have the problem like disease, like high blood pressure and heart trouble, sugar diabetes, like that. As far as I can remember, everybody healthy."

—*Joe Dan Osceola*

Traditional Food

Mealtime at Chestnut Billie's Camp

These women sit near the fire that consists of five logs forming a star shape. From left to right are Maggie Billie Buster, Mona Billie, Mona's sister (name unidentified), Pauline Tiger, Ruby Billie Clay, and Emma Tiger. The center where these logs meet is where the fire is set and as it burns, the logs are moved toward the center. On this fire the women cooked the food, which consisted of a wide variety of items such as corn, venison, rice and gravy, duck, garfish, and sweet potatoes. Pumpkins were also cooked in much the same way as potatoes are cooked today. Seminole pumpkins were different from the white man's pumpkins. They were grown in shady places and allowed to run up the trunks of big trees, where they ripened as much as fifty feet off the ground.

Women would often sing songs over the fire to summon an animal spirit to protect the fire, as they waved their hands gently over the flame. The old matriarchs believed that Seminoles must understand their place in the order of things and observe the traditional ways. As the owners of the family camp, the women would decide the location of the camp as well as when or if it should be moved. (Snellings Collection)

"If you put your fire out when you go to the next camp, it will be there when you return. You don't see the ashes, you don't see the flame, but it is there because you used the medicine before you left. Use this song and medicine will keep your family together..."

—*Susie Jim Billie*

Palmettos

Palmettos similar to the ones seen in this old postcard have a wide variety of uses among the Seminoles. They use the fronds to make the thatched roofs of the chickees. The trunks are used for the frames and platforms of the chickees. Twine made from the bark fibers was used to make rope and hair for the dolls for which the Seminoles have become so famous. The tender interior of the tree is used to make "swamp cabbage," a delicacy among the Tribe. (Snellings Collection)

Swamp Cabbage Recipe
from Cowbone (Paul Buster)

Source: Taken from the heart of the Sabal Palm tree

Process:
1. Chop the tree down
2. Strip all the stalks off the tree
3. Strip the bark of the tree lengthwise. Depending on the age of the tree, it may take 2 to 4 times doing this.
4. Cut it until the tender, fleshy, whitish, greenish part is exposed.
5. Slice, cut in chunks, or mince depending on cooking preference.

Cooking: It may be prepared as soup with ham, sofkee, milk shake or sautéed.

Traditional Food

Traders

Ted Smallwood opened a trading post in 1906 in his home and later moved it to a location at the water's edge. The store carried all the staples needed by the Indians and served as the local Post Office. The shallow water of that area was ideal for the Seminole's hand dugout canoes, and they traded there regularly. Mr. Smallwood ran the store until 1941, when he retired. It is still in operation today and a visit there is like stepping back in time to the days when this area of Florida was remote.

Smallwood traded with the Seminoles at his store in Chokoloskee (Indian name for "old house"). The Indians would bring gator, deer and otter hides, venison, turtle, turkey, and fish to trade for such items as coffee, flour, sugar, grits, and cloth. In earlier days, some of the most significant items of trade by the British were calico shirts and silver gorgets. Smallwood was well liked by the Seminoles, and he was one of the few whites who spoke their language.

Tourists and Florida history buffs can visit the store today at its original location. Much care has been taken to preserve and restore this part of Florida lore that was so important to the Seminoles in the early part of the twentieth century. It is one of the oldest buildings in southwest Florida.

It was often traders, during the late nineteenth century, who gave the Indians their English names. Consequently, we have today's prominent last names like Billie, Tommie,

The Smallwood Store

This is the Smallwood Store at Chokoloskee, Florida, where the Seminoles used to trade their hides and furs for supplies. (Snellings Collection)

Tiger, Doctor, John, etc. (Seminoles did not give out their Indian names to strangers.) Many of these same traders provided the opportunities for much of the cultural exchange between Indians and whites.

Ted Smallwood

Ted Smallwood stands on the steps of his store/trading post. (Snellings Collection)

7

Clothing and Style

Seminoles are famous for their colorful patchwork clothing and beads.

William Bartram, in his *Travels and Other Writings* (Literary Classics of the United States, Inc.), gave one of the best descriptions of the way Seminole women dressed during the eighteenth century:

> "They have no shirt or shift, but a little short waistcoat, usually made of calico, printed linen, or fine cloth, decorated with lace, beads, etc. They never wear boots or stockings, but their buskins reach the middle of the leg. They never cut their hair, but plat it in wreaths, which are turned up, and fastened on the crown, with a silver broach, forming a wreathed top not [sic], decorated with an incredible quantity of silk ribbons of various colors, which stream down on every side, almost to the ground."

Prior to the twentieth century, men wore breechcloths, sometimes with a shirt and boots or moccasins. A tailored hunting coat was often worn which was made of animal hide. Leggings were also worn by the men that were made of deerskin, cotton duck or wool, and they were buttoned at the ankle and held in place by a strap under the shoe. Men also wore turbans on their heads that were sometimes decorated with egret plumes or feathers from the great blue heron. Important men in the Tribe sometimes wore a silver band around the turban. Warriors often wore only a breechcloth and painted themselves with red and black paint.

Since the twentieth century, men traditionally wore a full-cut shirt down to the knees. An often colorful wool turban was worn on the head. Sometimes the man would also wear a vest, gorgets (large silver pendants) or other decorative items.

Seminole women's clothing has traditionally consisted of a full-length cotton skirt that was gathered at the waist and adorned with a ruffle near the knee. Blouses had long sleeves but were quite short, barely covering the breasts. Many strands of colorful beads were worn around the neck. During the early part of the twentieth century, patchwork clothing came into their culture, yet the same basic design was maintained. Thin, see-through, over-the-shoulder, waist-length capes of various colors, trimmed with a ruffle, were added to their wardrobe. As well as being decorative, these capes helped ward off mosquitoes.

Today, both men and women wear the popular patchwork items of clothing, such as vests, jackets, shirts, blouses and dresses. Patchwork also now extends to such items as holders for hot dishes and pans, pillowcases, and jackets intermingled with blue denim. And, yes, almost all now wear blue jeans.

Rosie and Sallie Billie

These two beautiful Seminole women display the colorful patchwork dresses that are made today. Many of these dresses have unique designs on them, some of which are on display at Ah-Tah-Thi-Ki Museum at the Big Cypress Reservation. (Snellings Collection)

Clothing and Style 81

Old-style Patchwork

Jane Motlow is seen in this extremely rare postcard sewing the patchwork clothing on her Singer sewing machine, while wearing one of the finest examples of the old style patchwork. Sinew and bone awl were first used to do the sewing before the introduction of steel needles and thread. Note the tremendous amount of glass beads around her neck. Some individuals had more than 200 strands of beads around their necks that covered the neck from the ears down to the breasts. Some accounts of this practice say that the women took them off at night in a carefully arranged fashion, while others reported that the women did not take off the beads even at nighttime. (Snellings Collection)

On the patchwork clothing are many signs or symbols that indicate things that are found in nature such as the turtle, lightning, rain, bird, tree, fire, crawdad and others. These symbols are sometimes connected with the stories and myths that are passed down from the elders. According to Betty Mae Jumper, these designs were not given names until recent years (probably during the 1940s, with the help of Deaconess Bedell).

"The jackets like this are more popular than ever before. What's so unique about Seminole Indian jackets is that nobody else on the face of the earth makes these kinds of jackets."

—Joe Dan Osceola

Seminole Matriarch, Squirrel Jumper

Squirrel Jumper — one of the matriarchs of the Tribe during the mid-twentieth century. She is holding Sallie Billie. (Snellings Collection)

Miccosukee- (Mikosuki-) speaking women began the art of patchwork clothing (*taweekaache*) around the time of World War I. It later spread to the Muskogee-speaking women near Lake Okeechobee. The process consists of sewing pieces of solid colored cloth together to make rows of designs that are then joined horizontally to another piece of fabric to make the garment.

Until the mid-twentieth century, Seminole women wore huge amounts of beads around their necks that are said to have weighed as much as 25 to 30 pounds. The beads were removed periodically for washing, but the women were seldom seen without them. Some say that the more beads a woman wore around her neck, the more beautiful she was considered to be. By the middle of the nineteenth century, some Seminole women had worn heavy amounts of beads until they developed severe neck and shoulder problems. Today's Seminole women still wear the beads, but usually only a few strands.

Men were known to wear beadwork, too. A diamondback rattlesnake motif was embroidered on a man's garter that was excavated at the Fort Brooke cemetery. Around some areas of southern Georgia near the Okefenokee Swamp, the timber rattlesnake, also known as the canebrake rattlesnake, is referred to as the "Seminole rattler."

"There was a set (of beads) that you put on top, but there was a set you had to wear at nighttime. They would take part off and leave part on; you're not supposed to be without anything around your neck. When we started wearing civilian clothes they told us we had to wear a necklace or something."

—Laura Mae Osceola

Clothing and Style

Seminole Beads

Squirrel Jumper (Billie Tommie Jumper) is shown in this postcard with many strings of colorful beads around her neck. Wearing this many beads involved a lot of care and effort. A Seminole woman, upon waking in the morning, would take the beads in graduated bunches from a basket where she stored them during the night and place them around her neck. She would then tie them together with a string. At night, after all of the day's work was done, the process was simply reversed.

Gifts by courting males would almost surely include strings of beads. (Snellings Collection)

Seminole Views

A Sewing Lesson

Lucy John gives a young lady a lesson in sewing the patchwork clothing. The Singer sewing machine was an important item in the lives of the Seminoles; it enabled the women to do embroidery and to make the fabulous patchwork clothing for which they are internationally known. It was a man named Me-le who was the first Seminole to use this machine in 1880. The art of sewing the patchwork clothing started sometime in the 1920s. (Snellings Collection)

"If you have a gift, then you will continue to be given. Pass it from generation to generation. Every time you lose gifts the world will change."

—Bobby C. Billie

Martha Willie

Busy making patchwork clothing, as little Virginia Mitchell (Bert, at the time this postcard was made) looks over her shoulder. Virginia is now the editor of the *Seminole Tribune*. (Snellings Collection)

Clothing and Style

Virginia Mitchell, editor of the *Seminole Tribune*, seen as a little girl in the previous postcard, looks a little different today. She is a Miccosukee- (Hitichi-) speaking Seminole who spent much of her early life living in the Everglades. She later went to live at the camp of Martha and Sam Willie on the Tamiami Trail. Virginia was educated in the public school system of the city of Miami. This is a classic example of the clash of two vastly different cultures that many Seminoles had to endure and it is living proof, in this case, of how adaptable the Seminole people are. In this photo, Virginia and her granddaughter, Shelli Osceola, are participating in a clothing contest at the "Seminole Days" festival in Chokoloskee, Florida, on March 28, 1998. Determination, strength, and courage are known to be characteristics of the Seminoles; talent and good looks can be added to that list, as well.

(Courtesy of Virginia Mitchell)

"The most valuable lesson taught to me was my language as a first language. I valued this because my grand parents did not speak English as well as they never went to school. They encouraged me constantly to go on with my education for I will be rewarded for that one day and to always help my people when they asked me for help.

"I was happiest growing up in the Indian village of Martha and Sam Willie in the Everglades. I treasure all that they taught me as a young girl and as a woman. There is not a day goes by that I don't think about how comfortable life was.

"Today I am teaching the same to my grand children and emphasize daily the importance of a good education to survive in this modern day world."

—*Virginia Mitchell*

Seminole Views

Louise Billie

In this recent postcard, Louise Billie is working on the beautiful patchwork clothing for which she is so well known. Seminoles did not always wear such colorful and elaborately designed clothing; women in the seventeenth century often wore tunics made of Spanish moss, which covered them from head to foot. (Snellings Collection)

Seminole Patchwork and Beads

Mary Osceola is dressed in a colorful patchwork outfit complete with many strands of beads around her neck. (Snellings Collection)

Clothing and Style

Traditional Seminole Hairstyle

This postcard shows the way traditional Seminole women used to fix their hair. Few still do that today. Until about 1900, Seminole women wore their hair in a tight bun on the top of their heads and it was only let down in times of mourning. In the 1920s women began to comb their hair forward toward their foreheads. They put a roll of cloth behind the hair and then flipped it back over the cloth at which time they pinned their hair down or put on a hair net (usually displaying beads in the net). During the 1930s cardboard replaced the roll of cloth, giving their hair a unique shape. Some tourists thought they were wearing hats, but it was only hair. In the 1940s and 1950s Seminole woman began to wear their hair similar to non-Natives. (Snellings Collection)

Ruby Smith

She is wearing many strings of beads, which was customary for Seminole women before the latter part of the twentieth century. Some of the elders still wear them regularly. Ruby also has her hair done in the old traditional way; this too has given way to today's more modern hairstyles. The Ah-Tah-Thi-Ki Museum staff reports that, in the old days, Spanish moss was sometimes rubbed into the hair as medicine to make it thicker. (Snellings Collection)

Mittie Osceola Jim

Shown in this postcard making traditional patchwork clothing. (Snellings Collection)

Royal Palm Hammock Style

Henry Jumper, Tommie Jumper, Ruby Billie, Squirrel Jumper (holding Billy Cypress) and friends pose for the photo used in this postcard at Royal Palm Hammock. (Snellings Collection)

Clothing and Style

89

Musa Isle Style

Mittie Osceola Jim, Annie Doctor Jimmie, Lena Osceola Billie, Annie Billie, Micky Tiger, and Maggie Billie Buster show off some beautiful outfits at Musa Isle in the 1930s. The clothing of the earliest Indians in Florida were not colorful and intricately made like the examples shown above, but mainly consisted of scant clothing that was made of vegetable fibers or animal skins and fur. Earlier tribes (such as the Calusa) used bone, stone and shells for ornamentation. (Snellings Collection)

Early Styles

Yupefushket (English name not known), third from the left, and his relatives show off their colorful clothing in this early postcard. (Snellings Collection)

"Seminole Squaws Making their Colorful Clothing"

Once again the demeaning term "squaw" is used to describe the women making their traditional clothing. Nevertheless, these women have become known the world over for the colorful dresses, vests and jackets that they made. As far as division of labor is concerned, until the middle of the twentieth century, the women made clothes and pottery, cooked the food and dressed the animal skins. The men hunted, traded, built canoes and fought the wars. (Snellings Collection)

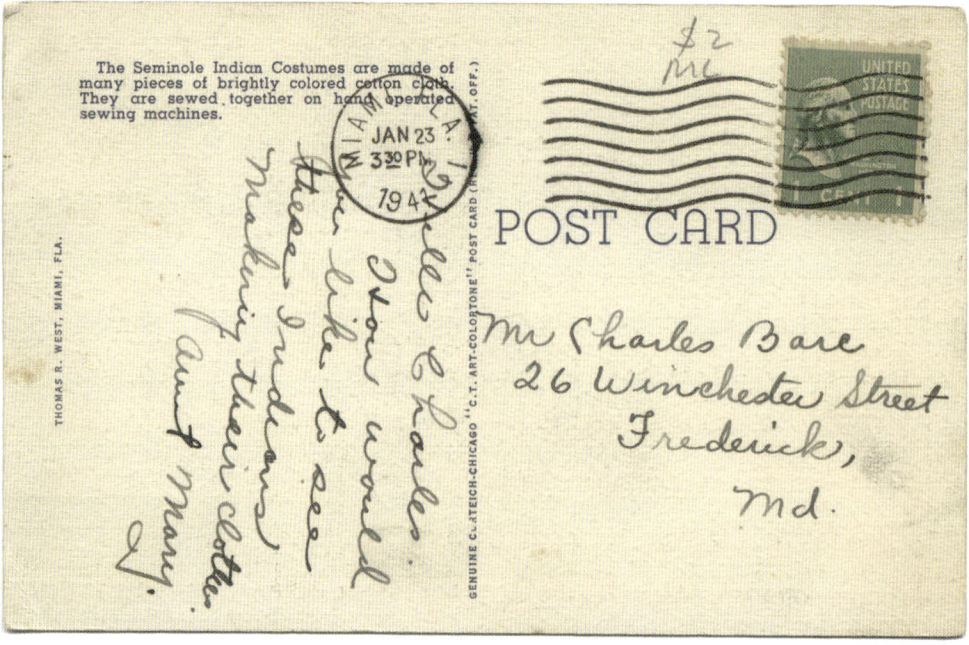

Reverse of the above-shown card.

Clothing and Style

91

Seminole Headdresses
This card, colorized in Germany, shows the Seminoles with several types of headdress. (Snellings Collection)

Casual Dress
A family more casually dressed, yet their clothes are still colorful. (Snellings Collection)

Desiree Jumper

The reigning Miss Teen Sugar in 2000 and the 2001 Miss Florida Seminole. (Courtesy of the *Seminole Tribune*.)

Cristine McCall,
Miss Florida Seminole 2005–2006

(Snellings Collection)

8

Transportation

Canoes were the main transportation for the Seminoles until the 1930s.

Eighty-seven sites where old canoes, many of which (53) have been carbon dated to be 500 to 5,000 years old, were discovered in May, 2000, at Newnan's Lake (an area called *chua* by the Indians, which meant "little jug with no bottom"). The lake is in north Florida at a place the Seminoles call *Pithlachocco* ("place of long boats" or "place where boats are made"). These canoes ranged in length from 15 to 31 feet. Many had what archeologists call "thwarts," which were raised areas in the center of the canoe to enable the paddler or poler to brace himself. Ironically, Newnan's Lake bears the name of a nineteenth century Indian fighter, Major Dan Newnan. It is the largest cache of prehistoric Indian canoes ever found and represents over one-fourth of the total number found in North America.

Many of these sites were severely damaged recently by a man on a bulldozer conducting what is known as "deadhead logging," which is the process of removing old submerged logs from the bottom of lakes and rivers. In this case there was total disregard for Native American artifacts and their history in general, not only by the logger, but also by the

The Bookmatched Grain of a Modern Seminole Canoe

Created by legendary canoe-builder, Henry John Billie, this canoe shows the intricate matching of the wood grain. (Snellings Photo)

regulatory agencies that were supposed to be the watchdogs for activities such as this. And not to be left out, some historians and anthropologists once again disagree as to the connection of these canoes to the ancestors of the present day Seminoles.

Cypress canoes were the main mode of travel for Seminoles during the nineteenth and early twentieth centuries. In addition to traveling to locations of trade and from one village to another, the canoes were used extensively for hunting and fishing. They were hand-carved from huge logs, using an assortment of tools, such as axes and handmade tools similar to an adz or a small mattock.

The canoes ranged from 24 to 30 inches wide and were up to 35 feet long, with large bows to part the surf and wide sterns to mash down the sawgrass. According to Bobby Henry (medicine man and canoe-maker), the old canoes were about five feet wide and 30 feet long. A canoe that was 25 feet long would weigh 700 pounds or more. Many of the most recent canoes were hand-sanded, and the resulting bookmatched grain of wood makes them very beautiful. Designed to last a lifetime, some are still around that were made more than a century ago. A few of the large ones made in recent years have sold for as much as $8,000.

"I fished for gar, mullet, and bass in canoes when I lived in the Everglades years ago. We carried everything in them: people, food, clothes, guns, and the dog. Sometimes the family would be gone for days at a time in the canoes to trade hides. I started carving tiny canoes and gifts from cypress with a pocketknife over sixty years ago. It was tough back then . . . I was ten years old before I ever saw a white man."

—Henry John Billie

Transportation

Those first sightings of the white man by Mr. Billie took place at Smallwood's store, where he used to make frequent trips by canoe with other Seminoles to get supplies. Henry John Billie passed away in 2004, leaving behind some of the remnants of his great works of art. Some of these items can be seen at the Ah-Tah-Thi-Ki Museum on the Big Cypress Reservation. With the passing of this great man, so passes the long era of the Seminole ancestors who made the hand-dugout canoes.

Henry John Billie learned the craft of building beautiful yet very functional works back in the '30s from his father and grandfather. He did the whole process from felling a giant cypress tree to the completion of the finished product. He is considered by all to be the master builder of these canoes and he knew more about them than anyone of his day; however, nobody is carrying on the tradition. What was once a vital skill has now faded from existence with his passing.

Building a Cypress Canoe

The late Henry John Billie was an acknowledged master canoe builder. (Snellings Photo)

The once open waterways have been filled and the canoes have been replaced with pickup trucks, helicopters and cars of every description. In fact, Henry John even participated in the building of some of the roads that cut off these same waterways once used by the Seminoles and their canoes. Ironically, he traveled to and from such work by poling his canoe.

In 1998, Henry John Billie received the prestigious Florida Folk Heritage Award for his canoe building. Anyone having seen his work can attest to his skill. Both his life and his work are treasured by the Tribe.

Hand-dugout canoes were the main transportation for the Seminoles in the 1920s. Frank Stranahan built a trading post at Fort Lauderdale, Florida, in 1901. Both he and his wife, Ivy, were staunch friends of the Seminole Indians. Mrs. Ivy Stranahan remembers seeing as many as 100 or so of these canoes coming down the river at one time, each one

Travel via Dugout Canoe

This is a colorful example of travel using a hand dugout canoe. These canoes were poled not paddled. This scene probably took place near the Tamiami Trail/U.S. Route 41. (Snellings Collection)

loaded with animal hides and hand made crafts to trade at the store.

Having made such a long journey, the Indians would sometimes stay in the area as long as a week. During this time they would buy and trade for pots, pans, cloth, salt, cooking oil, pipes, tobacco, beads, knives, grits, nails, flour, canned goods, guns, traps, axes, lard and a host of other things to make life in the 'glades a little more bearable.

The Stranahans considered the Seminoles to be good friends, and the Indians often had the run of their home. Mrs. Stranahan even held a school of sorts for any of the Tribe who would participate, especially the children. This school continued for 25 years until a federal day school was started at Dania in 1927. Mrs. Stranahan also made considerable effort to convert the Seminoles to Christianity and read them passages from the Bible on Sunday mornings. Mrs. Stranahan also organized a group called the Friends of the Seminoles, which was active in helping the Tribe.

Transportation

Cutting a Cypress Canoe

Josie Jumper and Frank Tommie work on a cypress canoe as Sam Huff observes. This mid-1950s postcard shows the two men making a "canoe trophy" for the University of Miami vs. the University of Florida football game. It is still on display at the Knight Sports Complex at the University of Miami. After completion, canoes used by the Tribe were often painted and decorated with great painstaking effort, indicating the families that owned them. (Snellings Collection)

Creating a Canoe from Cypress

Charlie Cypress is in the process of turning this cypress log into a large, hand-dugout canoe. (Snellings Collection)

Newly Completed Canoes

Cory Osceola, Chestnut Billie, Doctor Tiger, and Foosh Hatchet pose in this postcard with one of their newly completed canoes. (Snellings Collection)

Poling a Canoe

This is a perfect example of the canoes used in the eighteenth and nineteenth centuries. John Motlow (Matlow) is poling this one through an Everglades waterway. (Snellings Collection)

Transportation

Canoe with Sail Mast Raised

Canoes were often sailed in open water and across the Everglades during the nineteenth century. The sail was lowered when the canoes had to navigate narrow creeks and canals. This is one of the few postcards ever made showing the sail mast in an upright position.

Seminoles attacked the Dade County seat at Indian Key in 1840 under the command of Chakika, after crossing about 30 miles of open water in 28 canoes similar (though probably much larger) to this one. It was a feat that required great stamina and determination. (Snellings Collection)

A Family Outing

Roy Cypress takes his family for an outing in a cypress canoe. (Snellings Collection)

Seminole Views

Seminole Canoe on Taylor Bend

This scene takes place on Taylor Bend in the New River near Fort Lauderdale, Florida, back in the 1920s. The Seminoles called it the *Coontie hatchee*, named for the coontie plant that grew along the banks of the river. This plant was a source of food for the Indians. (Snellings Collection)

Canoe Maker, Henry John Billie

Canoe maker, the late Henry John Billie, poles a woman through the 'glades near Billie Swamp Safari on the Big Cypress Reservation. (Snellings Photo)

Transportation

Poling a Canoe

This card demonstrates how canoes were often heavily laden with people and supplies, and it also shows where the person with the pole stood. (Snellings Collection)

Guy LaBree Painted this Scene of a Seminole Poling a Canoe

LaBree is well recognized by the Seminoles and non-Indians alike for his ability to capture the essence of the Seminole on canvas. Known as "the barefoot artist" and a tough ol' Florida cracker, LaBree's paintings grace the homes of many Seminoles as well as the offices of Tribal officials. (Snellings Photo)

Their First Airplane Sighting

New modes of travel have become available to Native Americans now. In this postcard, a Seminole family appears to be seeing an airplane for the first time. (Snellings Collection)

Airboating

Eugene Tiger and Bobby Tigertail operate an old airboat for this postcard shot. This early model foreshadowed the powerful rigs that crisscross the Everglades today. (Snellings Collection)

Transportation

William Osceola

His airboat at full throttle across a remote section of the Everglades. (Snellings Photo)

"Harmony"
by Moses (Big Shot) Jumper, Jr.

The mystic cooing, I heard it

as I walked among the cypress

and willow tree.

At first I thought it was

my mind playing tricks on me.

But as the Breeze of the Gentle Wind

flowed through the glades

and softly touched my face.

I knew I was on Hallowed ground

and it was right for me

to be in this place.

Soon, the Hammock flowed with the phrases

of the Habitant's melody.

Each singing their songs of wit,

humor and mystery.

And for an instant,

I became a part of them

as they became a part of me.

Perhaps, if only for a moment, Harmony . . .

9

The Everglades

The River of Grass holds a special place in Seminole history.

The Everglades is a land of mood and mystery that can be both peaceful and unforgiving. Some of the most colorful characters in American history have been associated with it. This River of Grass holds a special place in Seminole history and has often been written about in novels such as Patrick Smith's *A Land Remembered* (Pineapple Press) and *Forever Island* (Pineapple Press). Many Tribal members are not happy with what is happening to the 'glades.

Wildlife was abundant in the Everglades prior to its draining and subsequent building of the Tamiami Trail that severed the great River of Grass forever; however, with the advent of these "improvements," Seminole men found themselves without a way to make a living. Men were basically reduced to some sort of oddity and often sat in a makeshift village as a spectacle for tourists. Self-esteem went to an all time low and, with all this time on their hands, some men embraced alcohol and antisocial behavior. In some cases, the men would get so drunk that the women would tie them up and take away their weapons until they sobered up.

106 Seminole Views

Indians Canoeing in the Everglades

The Seminoles have enjoyed, used and revered the Everglades for more than a century. They have hunted in it, fished in it, and reared their children in it. This old postcard shows children poling their hand-dugout canoe through the sawgrass. (Snellings Collection)

The days of hunting egrets for their plumes, and alligators, raccoons, otter and bear for their hides were but a fading memory. The loss of these things was especially hurtful to the Indians who live along the Tamiami Trail because they were neither interested nor trained in agricultural work. The Civilian Conservation Corps — Indian Division (CCC-ID) provided construction work for some of these men in projects that were themselves helping to destroy the Seminole way of life.

Decades ago, the men would divide into two groups of two or three, and their families moved into an area that deer were known to inhabit. Hunting was usually done during the early morning and late afternoon. The deer not sold at the trading posts were smoked and dried.

After WW I, the bottom fell out of the Florida boom market, and the depression of 1929 took its toll. The Seminoles then had much competition from white hunters, who killed game much more frequently and efficiently. Consequently, the Seminoles lost the big market they once had for animal hides, frog legs and palm hearts. Since this basically marked the end of this way of making a living, the Seminoles turned to the cattle and vegetable businesses to make a meager living.

The Everglades

Great Blue Heron, Bird of the Seminoles

The great Blue Heron has always had special spiritual significance to the Seminoles. In fact, there used to be a "Big Blue Heron" clan. (Snellings Collection)

"Birds have always been important to the Indian because they go where they wish, they light where they may, and they're free. We take these feathers from the birds. We use them in our ceremony because the feathers remind us of the Creator. The eagle flies highest in the sky of all the birds and so he is the nearest to the Creator, and his feathers are the most sacred of all. He is the highest of birds and so belongs to all tribes, to all peoples. And then each tribe has a lesser bird of its own. For the Seminole, it's the heron."

—*Buffalo Jim*

John Doctor — A Seminole, Fort Pierce, Florida

John Doctor (some say this is Doctor John and others say that it may be Doctor Doctor) is hunting in a palmetto thicket probably for deer. Hunters sometimes rubbed tobacco leaves on their guns and held them in the smoke of burning tobacco to bring good luck to the hunt.

Prior to 1907 only a name, address and postmark were allowed on the reverse side of the postcard. Any correspondence had to be done on the front. (Snellings Collection)

The Everglades

Home of the Seminoles, Pine Island, Fla.

Pine Island (Coyatalai) is of historical significance in that both Miccosukee and Seminole roots can be traced to it. Once secluded in the Everglades, it provided a major refuge for the Indians in which to live, hunt, and fish. Fort Lauderdale was established in 1838 so that military expeditions could be directed into Pine Island. In 1896 the railroad came and development began in Southeast Florida. As a result, the Indians were eventually chased out of the area. On February 22, 1990, Pine Island was officially designated as a Florida Historical Site. (Snellings Collection)

This scene shows one of the largest gatherings for a photo used in a postcard, showing Cory Osceola, Dan Osceola, Tom Billie and friends. (Snellings Collection)

Dredger at Work in the Everglades
(Snellings Collection)

The Destruction of the Everglades

The dredge changed the lives of the Seminoles around the turn of the century. Canals were built through the Everglades as early as 1880 through the initiative of a man named Hamilton Disston, and much of the water was gradually diverted or drained away. As a result, millions of acres of land were "reclaimed," and the 'glades became more accessible to non-Indians; so, thus began the encroachment on the Seminoles once again. Along with the dredging and the resulting retardation of the flow of this ever moving River of Grass, also came countless millions of mosquitoes to Seminole land.

"We have seen the people challenge the Creator's law from generation to generation. You can not overpower the Creator's law. You are a part of the creation, and you are destroying yourselves. You say you are doing this for the people and the younger generations yet to come. I don't think so, because what I see is nothing but roads, building after building, city after city. You need to stop and see what you are doing. The future is in the Mother Earth, the trees, the air, and the water, but if they are destroyed there is no nourishment for future generations."

—Bobby C. Billie

The Everglades

"There be more mosquitoes now, more than ever before due to one reason. But far as the mosquitoes go, they (Seminoles) use a mosquito net, a very thin material that people, natives found out they could use that, plus having a fire, smoke to keep the mosquitoes away. But why I said there's more mosquitoes out there, more than ever before, is due to the ecology, the drainage (lack of it), when there are a lot of fish, the mosquitoes lay their eggs in the water and the fish live off of that. Then the water got stagnated and there's hardly no fish, and the alligators eat up the fish and everything else, so that mess up the system. They didn't have too much mosquitoes before, but there's a lot out there now."

—Joe Dan Osceola

The Everglades Near Miami

In the days of the Spanish explorers during the late fifteenth century, the once eight-million acre expanse we now call The Everglades was a mysterious place and referred to by the Spanish as the "lagoon of the Holy Spirit." This truly vast area that was so awe inspiring is now threatened from all sides, which is lamented by many Seminoles. (Snellings Collection)

Even as early as 1830 there were people trying to drain the Everglades, as suggested by Dr. Perrine of South Florida. The U.S. General Jesup, who fought the Seminoles during the wars, wanted it drained for agricultural purposes. In 1928 the U.S. Army Corps of Engineers ignored the natural overflow of the 'glades and built dikes that resulted in tremendous loss of life in the

Seminole Views

The Big Tree

Huge bald cypress trees such as this fine example near Sanford, Florida, shown in this 1940's postcard were common in the eighteenth century before they were logged out. Some Seminoles lament the loss of these giants. (Snellings Collection)

great hurricane of that year. They also tried to straighten the Kissimmee River that was a meandering body of water that filtered fertilizer, pesticides and other pollutants, and provided habitat for many forms of wildlife. The result of that debacle was endless siltation and pollutants feeding into Lake Okeechobee and the Everglades from the land upstream. In 1928 the construction of the Tamiami Canal ended the free flow of water across the whole Everglades. It also ended the way of life that the Seminoles were used to when game was plentiful and the supply of fish seemed endless. Now the old canoe routes are choked with weeds, mosquitoes breed by the billions and the old stands of hardwood forest are gone.

To the traditional Seminole, the land is sacred and should not be owned by anyone; it's sort of like owning a parcel of air. You might use it, but that doesn't mean you're entitled to it. Thus, the concept of reservations does not set well with them. Modern developers — with their massive destruction of the earth, networking of roads and high-rise buildings—are appalling to the Seminoles; therefore, those who have never accepted "government land" are considered by the traditionalists to be the *real* Indians.

"Loggers started coming in and logging all the big trees and there are no more big trees, maybe just a few left. We don't want to cut anymore big trees. We want to make some canoes, but we don't want to kill the life of the elders of that area . . . Trees are still growing today, but without their elders they don't get big because they don't know what to do . . . We want to respect them. There is just a few left. The white people cut the rest down."

—*Bobby C. Billie*

The Everglades

Dredging a Canal in the Everglades
(Snellings Collection)

"We want to be free to hunt and fish as we always did, to live here without restrictions or red tape. We want no attachment to the federal government, and no help from it. That is our right. We don't want land — not the way white people want it. We don't believe in ownership of a certain area, and we don't have a claim, but one of these days we may be forced to make one . . . the name has changed, but we have always been here, we have never changed; it is those others who have gone away."

—*Guy Osceola*

"Most of the wetlands, the lakes, the rivers are very important to all life. Even if you don't acknowledge those things and think it's just a wasteland, I'll say it again, the wetland and the swamps is not a wasteland. It creates rain. Sometimes you feel the cold breeze come through and it hits your face and it makes you feel good, it's the wetlands that cool the air and it cleans the water and air for us. The wetlands and swamps and trees are the earth's cooling system. What we (the Seminoles) see the wastelands today, to us, is a four-lane highway going across the wetlands and swamps."

—*Bobby C. Billie*

(Snellings Photo)

The Florida Panther

Florida's state animal is the endangered Florida panther (*Coowahchobee*); however, it is much more than that to the Seminoles. It represents the guiding spirit during time of battle and is said to be the source of the most powerful medicine. Panther claws have been taken into battle by Tribal leaders and have been part of the "medicine bundle" of the Tribe's medicine men. It was used in secret ways to treat the wounds of war. Many things are kept in secret from the non-Indian and this relationship between the panther and the Seminole is a closely guarded one. Should the Florida panther cease to exist, it would be considered a serious loss for the Tribe.

The Everglades

(Snellings Collection)

"I don't know if it's medicinal but it's a spiritual thing. When God created earth, one of His favorite animals was this cat; he would put his head on His lap and He would pet it, and as you know, when the Creator touches things, and keeps His hand on it a little longer than normal somehow the electrical charge from His body goes into whatever he touches and becomes medicine . . . The panther was one of His favorite animals, so He would always pet him. Somehow word trickled down all these years, so like in the time of battle you wanted the most powerful thing to be at your side, so they would literally take the animal, they would eat the body and carry his robe or his skin into battle to let them know you got power. Its claws were used like basic acupuncture, particularly what you call the hang claw. That claw there, you ever see animals jump up on something they would go like this and they said the animal is like a panther, lion or whatever it is, they look like this and they look like they're grabbing them but sometimes this little extra one, when he comes back would rip them a little bit more, so they like to take that hang claw, pierce around them and actually pierce the skin to extract blood. The tail was used for male erection for a tickler, and then the rest of the body it has different flavors, it's got otter, bear, manatee, even tortoise. Like one time I killed one, when I first brought it back the old timers would gather and we skinned the animal. The first incision we used a knife but the rest of the incision was taking the hide off just with a thumb and nothing else."

—James Billie

Much research is being conducted to try to save this endangered part of Florida's natural community; however, the methods presently being used don't always meet with Tribal approval.

"The thing is, he (the panther) never truly adapts to that (biological research efforts) because that's unnatural and the second thing what it does to him, it makes the animal react unnatural. So he would never really do anything that he would do if he was just out there meandering around on its own. He now has an off pattern of what would be normal to him in the wild. I think you can study a lot of wildlife through science, through territories and through incidental sightings and all, but to have to go in and traumatize an animal, treeing him up inside a big (cypress) head and then having to sedate him to get him down and put a collar and tag on him, again that's an interruption of nature. Another thing too is that evolution has a way of taking care of itself, regardless of the fact that they are inbred or whatever, they still have their natural instincts to survive and to be an animal. I think the way evolution works is, it will adapt, it's Mother Nature's way, and if there's enough of them and you leave them alone . . . I mean look at the Seminoles, when we had only 200 members that was left here back in the swamps years ago, and now we're up close to 3 or 4,000 people, including the Miccosukees and everybody around, do you realize how many in that little group were relatives? They were the same as these panthers out here."

—Danny Tommie

The Everglades

(Snellings Collection)

The fact is that Seminole land and the adjacent Big Cypress Preserve may be the only area vast enough that has suitable habitat for this magnificent animal to survive. Water levels and the availability of food are constantly changing in the panther's range, so a huge area (as much as a hundred square miles) is needed for the cat to survive.

". . . They (wildlife) are not animals to us, they are the first born of this earth. They never changed their way of life. You might call them animals, but they know what the God given life is. They won't change that. That's how they are supposed to live on this earth. All of those little things, the natural creations have something to do with our life. Even (if) you don't acknowledge them, they acknowledge you . . . They have no voice to tell you to stop taking away their homes. But Indigenous People also speak for those that have no voice. They are the first born of the earth."

—Bobby C. Billie

The Legend of the Panther and the Rattlesnake

The panther and the rattlesnake came across each other in the forest one day. They looked at each other and finally the panther said to the rattlesnake, "I am the most dangerous animal in the forest. With my strength and my claws I can tear you apart."

The rattlesnake looked at the panther and said, "I don't think so. I am the most dangerous animal in the forest. With my fangs, one bite from me and I will put venom deep in your veins from which you will not recover."

The panther said to the rattlesnake, "Alright, I'll go up in this live oak tree and stay and not eat. You stay down here at the bottom of the tree and not eat and we will see who can last the longest and the winner is the most dangerous animal in the forest." The rattlesnake agreed and the panther went up to the top of the tree.

A few days passed and the panther hollered down to the rattlesnake, "Are you still down there?" The rattlesnake shook his rattle loudly so the panther would be sure to hear.

Two weeks passed and the panther was getting hungry and he called down to the rattlesnake, "Are you still down there?" The rattlesnake shook his rattle loudly so the panther would be sure to hear.

In another week or so the panther came down from the top of the live oak tree and said to the rattlesnake, "I think we can agree, we are both the most dangerous animals of the forest." . . . and they went their way in peace.

—Cowbone

The Everglades

An Old Swamp Buggy

This old swamp buggy is a forerunner of the big rigs that crisscross the Everglades and swamps today. (Snellings Collection)

"You got all these weekend warriors who call themselves hunters who look forward to this hunting season and they get out there and all they do is go out there to booze, to trash up, to take these mud buggies around . . . you see these big old buggies going out there, and what they're doing is rutting up the Everglades and then when you take fifty of those buggies and they're running all over out there, and they're spilling oil, they're dropping transmission fluid, they're going through (cypress) heads that they don't need to be in and the next thing you know, you can't find anymore natural orchids that grow out there, all these sensitive things you know. You're going to see cypress trees, but if you walk into a natural cypress habitat, and the people know what they're looking for, they can see a lot of the wonders of nature right there, but you can't see a lot of that no more because a lot of that has been destroyed . . . now the state and federal agencies want to step in and buy up the properties, and you got good people that's part of the Big Cypress Preserve right now that's established a home and living out there, and so when they came in and bought this and turned this into part of the Federal Preserve, now they want to force these people to leave their homes. But yet they've opened it up for years to thousands of outsiders to come in and do what they want . . ."

—Danny Tommie

Artist's Scene of the Everglades

There have been several artists in the Seminole Tribe who have achieved notoriety with their talent. These include such artists as the late Noah Billie and Henehayo Osceola. (Snellings Collection)

Medicine

The power of Seminole cures is said to come from within the medicine man or woman.

There are many plants and herbs that have had a host of uses for the Seminoles over the centuries. For example, the live oak tree (*Quercus virginiana*) provides medicine for back pain and post-menopausal ailments. The shoestring fern (*Vittaria lineata*) helps cure depression and is also used when lightning strikes near a person. The cabbage palm (*Sabal palmetto*), as well as providing food, is said to help high blood pressure. Brazilian pepper (*Schinus terebinthifolius*) has been used to treat tumors, ulcers, and as an antiseptic and aphrodisiac. Poison ivy (*Toxicodendron radicans*) was used in the nineteenth century to treat rheumatism, liver disease and paralysis. Some of the Seminole uses for poison ivy are unsaid. The strangler fig (*Ficus aurea*) is used by the Seminoles to heal cuts and scrapes by applying the leaves as bandages. Sassafras (*Sassafras albidum*) is used to cure such things as horse sickness, opossum sickness, otter sickness, wolf sickness, and sore throats and coughs. None of these remedies is deemed effective without the chants and songs that go with them. Power is said to come from within the medicine man or woman.

Seminole Views

Seminole Child with Medicine Pouch

A medicine pouch hangs from the neck of this unknown Seminole child as he plays with toy drums. In traditional custom, male babies have their hair ceremonially shaved when they are four months old, leaving only a forelock, such as the one on this child, depicted in an early postcard. (Snellings Collection)

There are also many ailments, for which the Seminoles have medicine, that are not known to or treated by the non-native world, such as lizard sickness, gopher tortoise sickness, water people sickness, scalping sickness, ghost sickness, grass sickness, thunder sickness and a host of other difficulties. Seminole medicine is quite extensive, to say the least, and it takes the practitioner many years of study under a medicine man or woman to learn the profession. There is not room in this text to cover all of the aspects of Seminole medicine, even if the medicine men or women decided to reveal all of the information — something that they do not do.

Warriors were said to be able to turn into some sort of plants, making them indistinguishable from the bushes and thereby making them invisible to their enemies. The Oconee (possibly Cowkeeper's band) were said to have used this practice.

"It's (the medicine pouch) mostly for protection and to make babies safe. It's made of herbs. They keep it on a necklace or sometimes they put it on a little bracelet."

—Jeanette Cypress

Medicine

Medicine Men

The men in this postcard were four of the most prominent medicine men of the Tribe during the early twentieth century: Bill Motlow, Tom "Homespun" Billie, John Willie and Cory Osceola. Few men are willing to undertake the apprenticeship of seven years that is required to learn all of the medicines, songs and chants required to be a medicine man. Much dedication and sacrifice is needed for this intense learning process. Medicine men and women are not paid in cash; they are paid with gifts. According to the practitioners, they did not pay for the skills that they have, so they will not take any money — only gifts. (Snellings Collection)

"When I got older I studied with my uncles. Nothing is written down; you have to memorize the teachings. The reason they memorize everything is because we were told the white people were going to be here for a long time. First the French, then the Spanish, and they were just as hungry for what we knew as the white people are today. Our healers felt that they didn't want these people to take everything from us, so they made the information non-readable. You have to memorize it yourself; your head becomes like a book . . ."

—Sonny Billie

Susie Jim Billie

At a little more than 100 years old (at the time of this photo), Susie Jim Billie, renowned Seminole medicine woman from the Big Cypress Reservation, practiced her profession and she would go into the woods in search of plants and herbs that she used. Four of her five children were born in the swamp where she went to give birth alone. The fifth one was born in a hospital; she said that one was the worst experience of the five. Granddaughter Jeanette Cypress says Susie Jim Billie lived to be 106–108 years old. (Snellings Photo)

Medicine

"Susie Jim Billie was the matriarch of five generations with eight children, 26 grandchildren, 45 great grandchildren and 18 great-great grandchildren — and still counting. According to census records, Susie was approximately 102 years old at the time of her passing, but like so many of the Seminole ancestors before her, Susie was born in the woods of Florida where no medical records were transcribed. Therefore, oral history becomes our only record, and with that we are able to place her age more closely to 108 years at the time of her passing. Susie resided on the Big Cypress Reservation in Florida, where she cared for her youngest surviving son with Down's syndrome, Pilot, who was 60 years old at the time of this writing. Susie was a remarkable woman, she lived unassisted well into 100 years of age; she lived through the turmoil that plagued the Seminole history, and her life had spanned the introduction of modern technologies into the Seminole culture. Her first plane ride took place when she was approximately 80 years old, and she was able to go to the Smithsonian to help identify Seminole artifacts.

Susie Jim Billie
(Snellings Photo)

"Susie was blessed and was thankful for the ability to heal through the traditional Seminole medicine. She was sought not only by her own people for her healing and wisdom, but by authors for books and by individuals across the country who had heard of her traditional healing powers. Although Susie spoke only the native language of her people, Miccosukee, and she had never received a formal education, we are so thankful because through her dedication to her culture and traditions, she passed on her knowledge like her ancestors before her had done. Therefore, she will remain an endless source of wisdom for the Seminole people."

—Daniele Jumper

Seminole Views

Bobby Henry

Bobby Henry, the medicine man from Tampa, is famous for his rain dances. He claims to have brought rain during times of drought to various stricken areas of Florida in recent years. (Snellings Photo)

Some medicine men believe that a large portion of disease is brought on by the loss of the soul. Many Seminoles believe in a double soul and that one soul may leave the body in the form of dreams, while the other soul stays with the body. To discover the cause of sickness it is believed that the medicine men must analyze the dreams.

Successful doctors and medicine men are said to have powerful medicine in their bodies. Accordingly, this medicine (or power) gives off a smell that is inhaled by the patient. This living medicine is said to make the practitioner capable of such things as passing through locked doors or making a virgin pregnant.

The Upjohn Pharmaceutical Company had been interested in Josie Billie's herb tea because the Indians said it cured "brain sickness." But Josie said, " It was not as strong as when it was used with songs (which are sung in a low voice) and fasting. The spirit of the medicine comes from inside the man who has the power." Instructions regarding Seminole medicine are quite specific and must be followed carefully.

When the sawmills opened in the Everglades in 1934, malaria became a problem among the Seminoles. Blacks were brought in from Georgia to work in the mills, and the mosquitoes spread the disease from the Blacks to the Seminoles. Prompt medical treatment cured the problem.

Medicine

Because of a diet of largely soft foods, pyorrhea became another problem for the Seminoles in the first half of the twentieth century. Large wooden *sofkee* spoons were regularly passed among the Tribe, thus spreading infections of various sorts. Pots and pans were not sterilized with hot water, or anything else, and sometimes were also a source of infection.

In recent decades the Seminoles have, for the most part, adopted the white man's medicine in case of serious illness. Only hospitals are equipped to handle some of the problems that have plagued the Tribe, such as high infant mortality rates (the highest among all Indian Tribes), tuberculosis and alcoholism.

Among the Seminoles is a well-known (even outside of the Tribe) rainmaker, Bobby Henry, at the Tampa Reservation. He explained a little bit about how and where he got started, but as might be expected, he will keep the songs and chants to himself.

"I started in the Everglades near what's now Alligator Alley. I was ten or eleven years old and I lived on the Tamiami Trail. Ingram Billie taught me what he knew to do when I was twelve years old because he wanted me to carry on after he was gone. The place where I learned it is where I was born near where Turner River road is today near Ochopee. Rain dance takes four days and I fasted for those days. You can't lie and you can't cheat. Rain benefits the earth, the animals, and all people."

—*Bobby Henry*

Interesting Reverse Sides of Seminole Cards from the Snellings Collection.

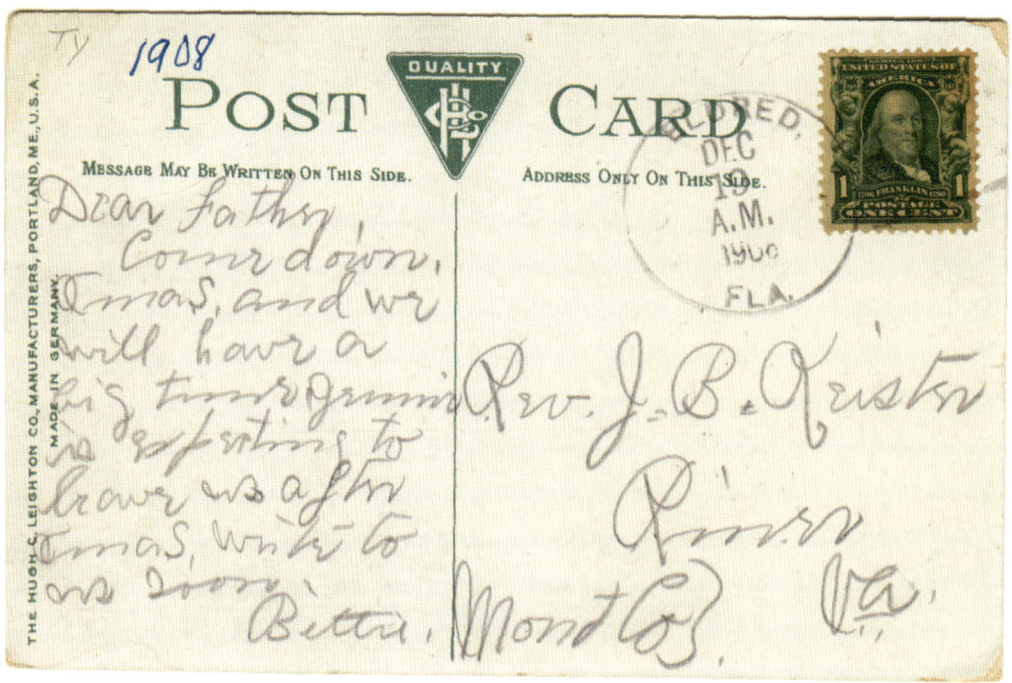

Religious Customs

Traditional Seminole beliefs hold that a person has two souls.

Some Seminole medicine men believe that the "Breathgiver" (God) lives in the sky and that He is linked to (but not the same as) the sun. Here on earth He is represented by the sacred fire. According to old Seminole ways, some do not believe in just one soul; they believe each person has two souls — one that stays with the body and one that wanders in the form of dreams. Both souls leave the body only upon death. The soul that wanders may encounter a soul of the opposite sex. In this case, that soul may not return to the body by dawn; therefore, the body awakens with sickness and a doctor or medicine person is called to follow the missing soul and bring it back to the body. If this medicine is not successful, then the person dies.

Historically, religious matters in the Seminole Tribe were attended to by the medicine men and elders of the Tribe. Today, a large portion of the Tribal members are Baptists. This transition was difficult and met with considerable resistance from the medicine men and women in the beginning. Even today religious practices might be what you could call "a bumpy road."

Green Corn Dance

Robert Osceola, shown in this postcard, is supposed to be leading the Green Corn Dance; however, it may be a reenactment at the Seminole Village in Hollywood for the benefit of tourists. During the Green Corn Dance the women wore rattles around their ankles. These rattles were made from box turtle shells that contained hard, sun-dried balls of mud, which made a lot of noise as they stomped their feet. If worn today, the dried mud in the shells has probably been replaced by nails (Snellings Collection)

The Green Corn Dance

The Green Corn Dance (*Shot Cay Taw*) is an event during which the clans come together to celebrate, play traditional games, dance, feast, energize the Tribe's medicine bundle, conduct Tribal ceremonies and mete out punishments to those guilty of crimes.

"Our Green Corn Dance is not a God that we worship, it's just the food that the Creator made for us to give us a sign that we are alive and we still have this food that He has given us. That's one of the main things that we know: that we have corn that Creator gave us in our legend so we would think that it's our home . . . this [the time of the Green Corn Dance] is when all creatures come together in harmony and celebrate the fact that the Creator is still with us, and his making of us, and that the ancient tongue is still being talked, and the ancient old festival dance still being danced."

—*James Billie*

Religious Customs

The date of the Green Corn Dance is set by the medicine man, usually from late April to early July, near the date of the new moon — when the green corn ripens. Once a month-long event, the event is now held over the course of a week. It is held in remote locations, and non-Indians are usually not welcome.

> "See, corn just lasts like four to five days. People get there early enough, it used to last about a month fifty or sixty years ago, because that's when they didn't have transportation. So that's the only time they see each other, once a year at the Corn Dance. So they would take part in the religious segment and socializing, the people they haven't seen for a year, so that's why they used to last about a month, but now only about a week, when the people start getting there."
>
> —*Joe Dan Osceola*

The Green Corn Dance became a very important part of Tribal life after the Seminole Wars, bringing an already dispersed group together with some semblance of unity and spiritual meaning. In fact, one of the main goals of the Green Corn Dance was to insure the Tribe's power in time of war.

Today the Panther and Bird clans are in charge of the festival (Panther and Wind clans for the Miccosukees). Eight Seminole clans still exist: Bear, Panther, Wind, Deer, Otter, Bird, Snake and Big Town, and each has its own camp at the Green Corn Dance. The women prepare food, and everybody has plenty to eat until the day of fasting comes, which lasts for thirty hours.

Traditional dances are also performed during this preparatory time. Many dances, songs, and chants exist among the Seminoles, though they are secretive about them. The alligator dance, catfish dance, hunting dance, chicken dance, screech owl dance, and many others have been passed down through the ages. At one time there were over 100 in all, and some have been lost. Medicine men like Josie Billie and Ingram Billie carried some of them to their graves.

There is much socializing during the Green Corn Dance, especially in the first two days while the grounds are being prepared. Stickball games are played at this time. The pole for the stickball game is located just outside the dance circle. It is made of a tall pine trunk, about twenty feet tall, with its branches trimmed off. The pole is hewn square about five feet off the ground and scores are kept using charcoal marks on that part of the pole. The ball is made of deerskin.

Both boys and girls play the game together with the men (boys against the girls) using the ball sticks to throw the ball and the women using their hands. In some of the games, only men play (sometimes using two sticks per person). The object of the game is to hit the pole with the ball. The first team to reach a stipulated number of points wins the game. The game serves as a release for youthful energy and to teach the young how to work together.

In the old days one town would challenge another, and the atmosphere was quite different. The game was so hard-fought that some players would be killed during the game and many others would be injured.

Stickball Scene by Mary Gay Osceola

Stickball is a game that some archaeologists believe dates back to the mound builders of about 900 A.D. Stickball is important as a model of appropriate behavior toward others. (Snellings Collection)

Stickball Game Ball

This is an example of the game ball used in the stickball contests held at the Green Corn Dance. This one was presented to author Patrick D. Smith by Tribal Chairman James Billie. (Snellings Photo)

Religious Customs

The tribal medicine bundle is always at the Green Corn Dance (the dance itself is held at midnight on the third day), and it is the focal point of all of the festivities. It is one of the most important items of the Seminole culture, since it is supposed to have power over almost all phases of Tribal life. The medicine bundle consists of many objects such as horn, herbs, snake fangs, minerals, stones and other things that the Indians believe to be essential for their well being. The Tribe believes that the Creator will reach down and put new medicine in the bundle at the end of the Green Corn Dance. The objects in the bundle are tied in their own little buckskin pouches and are kept in a deer hide. One of the main purposes of the Green Corn Dance is to keep alive the medicine in the Tribe's medicine bundle.

Prior to the Seminole Wars, there was only one bundle, but as warfare became menacing, it was divided into several bundles. In no other Tribe does the medicine bundle play such a significant role, binding together the cultural identity of the whole Tribe.

Historically, the bundle included medicine of war that made warriors powerful, such as the "thunder missile," which made them invisible to their enemies. Another medicine was said to enable the warrior to deflect bullets. Rattlesnake fangs were used to scratch the warriors, making them fearless and extra strong. Special flint was used to light the fire for the dance and it was kept wrapped in a cow horn.

> "During war time they [the medicine men] prepared certain medicine bundles. And this is like the Arc of the Covenant. The Israelites had an Arc of the Covenant to help them. Well, the medicine bundles were sometimes prepared for war to carry into battle for safety and to ensure victory."
>
> —*Billy Cypress*

A medicine man is always in charge of the medicine bundle, since the objects contained therein are said to be so powerful that any mishandling can cause the medicine to have a detrimental effect on the Tribe. It has been said that if the bundle turned on them, it could eat their blood, causing all sorts of ailments. Some medicines were considered too powerful to touch and were handled with buzzard wing bones. The medicine bundle is brought out on a special day for the Tribe — court day.

In the early nineteenth century during a Green Corn Dance, a Tribal leader (*Micco*) sat on the ground of the west side of the village square, surrounded by his advisors. The chief faced the east, because the sun played an important part in the religion of the Tribe. The warriors and the war speaker sat on the south side. Others sat on the east and north side of the square. The important officials of the Tribe could not eat or sleep until all matters to be brought before them were discussed.

Known today as "court day," it is a time when offenses committed by Tribal members are tried and punishments assigned. Punishment for offenses was quite severe in the Seminole Tribe, so even today crimes are few. "Criminals" are said to be out of their minds because they have not acted for their own good and, therefore, cannot participate in Tribal activities. They can take their place in the Tribe once again if they place themselves in the hands of the medicine man for rehabilitation. Legends have occasionally followed some individuals who were on the receiving end of punishment.

The court-day legend of "Crop-eared Charlie" (Charlie Tiger) tells of an Indian who had his ears cut off (some say the lobe of only one ear was cut off) as punishment because he was romantically involved with a woman who was of his own clan — a major offense among the Seminoles. He was then given a knife and banished from the Tribe (some say for one year, some say for many). A different legend about the same man says that he was punished thusly because, while drunk, he betrayed the Seminoles who murdered four settlers at New Smyrna on December 17, 1856.

"Scratching" is also performed at the Green Corn Dance. Scratching is used both as a mild form of punishment and as a symbol of purification. It is done either with needles that are placed in a wooden block or with a turkey or hawk quill. Both arms and legs are scratched, front and back. Babies are scratched only a little bit. No infections have ever been recorded from such scratchings.

Another purification ceremony involves drinking the "black drink" (*cassina*), a powerful mixture consisting of a host of ingredients, including snakeroot, the inner bark of the willow tree, leaves of the sweet bay, ginseng, wild grapes and the lizard's tail plant. The holly tree (*Ilex vomitoria*) is also used to make this drink, and the Indian name for it is *asi*. These plants are boiled into a strong, tea-like drink, and the Indians believe that the drinking of it, and the subsequent vomiting it induces, purifies them. Tribal members drink this mixture, and thus purge themselves of any poisons in their systems, and this helps purify their bodies.

Centuries ago, Tribal warriors would sit in a circle and perform a ceremony of drinking the black drink. Before they drank they would cry out, "*Asiyahola!*" The name of the famous Seminole warrior, Osceola, is said to have been derived from this long, drawn-out cry, although some members of the Tribe say that this is not true.

Names are given during the Green Corn Dance. A child is given a name, which may be changed when he grows older. If a person performs some great deed or courageous

Religious Customs

feat, he may be named yet again. Even English names were given to the Seminoles, and those names are familiar Seminole names, such as Billie, Tommie and Doctor.

> "When the child is like twelve or fourteen years old, they can go to the rituals [of the Green Corn Dance]. Nothing to eat for a day and a half, and at midnight they get a name."
>
> —Joe Dan Osceola

On the last day of the Green Corn Dance a medicine man goes to the medicine bundle at dawn to examine each little pouch to see if the emissary (*Este Fasta*) from God (*Hesackeeta Mesee*) has given them anything new. When he is finished, he picks up the medicine bundle and walks toward the east until he is out of sight. This bundle will not be seen by the Tribe again until the next Green Corn Dance. When the medicine man returns, empty-handed, the dance is over and a feast begins, including the eating of corn and other foods brought in by the women.

The Seminoles unknowingly fulfilled a Jewish law with the celebration of the Green Corn Dance:

> "And ye shall eat neither bread, nor parched corn, nor green ears, until the self-same day ye brought an offering to the Lord."
>
> —Leviticus 23:14

Modern day corn dances have seen changes, as have other aspects of Seminole culture. For example, women no longer wear turtle shell rattles filled with seeds of wild canna or dried mud on their legs to maintain cadence in the dances; they have been mostly replaced by tin cans filled with seeds or nails. Other changes include the absence of the cane flute, tobacco sacks made of pelican's pouches and sandals made of alligator hide.

Marriage

According to James Glenn, who worked with the Seminoles during the early part of the twentieth century, a Seminole marriage was quite simple at that time (contrary to what is depicted on the postcard on the next page). After both sides of the families involved have

A Seminole Wedding

This postcard depicts a Seminole wedding, and both sides of the family are represented. The background shows the presence of many white people, indicating this ceremony was probably staged. The two young Seminoles joined ring fingers as a symbol of their unity during the ceremony. Seminoles were not allowed to marry within their own clan. To do so meant swift and severe punishment. Some offenders were even whipped until they died. Adultery among women was not tolerated; severe punishment could result, including cropping of their ears or nose. Men, on the other hand, could take as many wives as they could support. The punishments have now been abandoned. (Snellings Collection)

approved of the marriage, a day is appointed for it to take place. At sundown on that day the man simply goes to the camp of the woman he is to marry and begins to live with her ever afterward. The contract is then concluded.

"In the old days, the groom goes to his future bride's mother's camp, usually accompanied by an uncle. The groom brings household items, presents from his family, a new gun, pots, pans and tools. The matriarch of the camp would eventually come out briefly and pronounce the couple husband and wife."

—*Ah-Tah-Thi-Ki Museum*

Religious Customs

According to Seminole custom, husband and wife go to live with the family of the bride's mother after the couple is married. The clan (*Pohapohumkosin*) is the basic family unit and descends from the mother. Seminoles believe that at the time of creation, the Breathgiver (God) made sixteen clans in order to keep their society together and the body strong. There are no favorites among the clans (though some are said to rank higher than others), but legend has it that the Bird Clan was the first. Some clans, such as the Alligator Clan, are gone now; only the Panther, Bird, Wind, Big Town, Deer, Otter, and Snake Clans remain.

Seminoles have intermarried with several different races of people, including whites, Blacks, and members of other Tribes. During the eighteenth century Seminole men would kill Yamassee Indian men and marry their women. Bartram noted in 1773 that the Seminole leader, Cowkeeper, also had Yamassee slaves. During the days before the Civil War, Blacks often sought refuge with the Seminoles and some intermarriage took place then. Some of the present day leaders of the Tribe are also of mixed blood, such as former Tribal Chairman James Billie (half white), Betty Mae Jumper (half white) and Sally Tommie (a Black Seminole).

Death

In the old days mourners would carry the well-wrapped remains of a dead Seminole to the burial site (usually in the wilderness on high ground) the same day of death if enough daylight was left. If not, they would go the day after.

A member of his or her own sex would wash the body of the deceased. When a husband died, women removed their necklaces and dressed in black and wore their hair in a single braid. Men did not cut their hair for four months after the death of a spouse and did not change clothes during this time. They broke the personal belongings of the deceased so that the spirits of those items could also make the journey to the spirit world.

A Seminole tomb usually consisted of pine logs about three feet high that were lashed together with grapevines. Sometimes they buried the deceased in a hollow tree.

A fire was built to scare off the "evil birds" and was kept burning for four days. The personal possessions of the deceased were also taken to the burial site, and a man's dogs or horses were taken there and killed so that they might go with him to the world beyond. A rare account of a traditional Seminole burial was given in 1896 by a renowned outdoor sportsman of that day, C. B. Cory, who had extensive contact with the Indians.

Seminole Indian Graves

The scene in this postcard is quite puzzling because no Seminole would ever allow himself or herself to be photographed at a gravesite. It would be interesting to know what the circumstances were in this case. (Snellings Collection)

"Upon the death of an Indian, the body is clothed in a new shirt, and usually a handkerchief is tied around his neck and a new turban put on the head. Sometimes the face is painted, usually with a round spot on the cheek. A piece of burnt wood is placed in the left hand and a bow and one arrow is usually buried with him. When the place for the burial is selected, the ground is prepared in the following manner: A floor of palmetto logs is built some seven feet long by three feet wide, over which a roof of palmetto leaves is constructed. The body is placed in this small house, the feet, it is claimed, are always placed toward the East. The body is usually wrapped in a blanket and covered with logs, forming kind of a box with the palmetto leaf roof over it. A fire is built at the end of the tomb, which is renewed at sunset for three days, and lighted torches waved about for a few moments to frighten away the 'bad birds.' After the third day the fires are allowed to go out."

—C. B. Cory

Religious Customs

The medicine men boiled roots and other medicine, and anyone who had contact with or tended to the dying person had to take a bath in this medicine and drink some of the mixture. Those present rubbed themselves in bay leaves after returning from the burial.

For four days the relatives of the deceased attend the burial site. Guns are fired into the air, a procedure that is said to prevent the soul from returning to the camp and subsequently taking another soul with him when he leaves the camp.

After a four-month period, restrictions are lifted and the grave is revisited and cleaned. When this is completed, the mourners leave and never return. According to custom, if a person died in one of the camps, that camp had to be abandoned; however, this custom is no longer strictly adhered to.

> "All my ancestors have been put away the natural way. We have been doing this way over six million years and that is our right. This is the Creator's law. We consider the taking of the ancestors and their belongings from the earth as something that violates the rights of all indigenous natural people. The burial grounds are resting places of our ancestors and should be protected and untouched. We consider all remains whether historic or prehistoric as ancient relatives which must be protected from any disturbance. The burial grounds which have been disturbed should be put back as they originally were and those items which have no safe place to be returned should be put back to earth in the right and respectful way, not in museums or sold as collector's items."
>
> —*Bobby C. Billie*

Today, Seminoles have mostly adopted the customs of the white man and funerals are usually held at churches and proceed in a traditional Christian manner.

Christianity

Deaconess Bedell, an Episcopal missionary, was instrumental in bringing Christian teachings about God (*Hisakitamisi*) to the Seminoles and in teaching them how to market their handiwork. While working in the 1930s at the Glade Cross Episcopal Mission at Everglades City, Florida, she visited the villages of the Seminoles, no matter how remote they were. She often walked or traveled by canoe to see the Indians. Some were reluctant

Deaconess Bedell

Episcopal missionary, Deaconess Bedell (The Seminoles called her Little Bird), poses with Wilson Cypress and friends for a photo postcard of her parishioners. (Snellings Collection)

to accept her when she first started working with the Tribe, which was not surprising considering the conduct of some missionaries who preceded her.

It was not uncommon for some missionaries to scoff at Seminole traditions, beliefs, festivals, language and even the clothes they wore. Surely teachings from the Bible must have been in there somewhere, but there is little evidence of anything but conduct contrary to the faith they were supposed to represent. In one instance in 1949 a male missionary beat three young Seminole women with an electric cord folded to four thicknesses. The offense? They had attended a dance with his son.

The attitude of Deaconess Bedell was to lift up the Seminoles, not tear down their heritage or demean their activities. By helping the Seminoles with the marketing of their handiwork and proving that their crafts were of good quality, the Deaconess also helped raise their self-esteem. Miss Bedell was of the opinion that the tourist attractions in the Miami area were not good for the Indians. She became quite vocal about the matter, speaking around the state to people who would listen saying that they were exhibited like "monkeys and alligators"; however, she never mentioned the fact that these camps in the

Religious Customs

attractions helped make the public aware of Seminole culture.

At that time there was little mentioned of the fact that the Seminoles were not there against their will. Somehow it always came back to the efforts of non-Indian cultures to make the Indians "assimilate" into the world of the white man. This fact does not negate all that Miss Bedell had to say, because thoughtless tourists would often make fun of the Seminole's clothes, make crude remarks and throw coins at the children. In such cases, though, we have more of a commentary on the culture of the non-Indian. Fortunately, there have been efforts to build upon the footsteps of Miss Bedell in recent years.

Willie King, a Creek Indian from Oklahoma, was one of the more influential missionaries to the Seminoles in the '30s and '40s. His efforts were eventually sponsored by the Home Mission Board of the Southern Baptist Convention. The work that Reverend King began, and which was continued by Reverend Stanley Smith, greatly accelerated the success of Baptists among the Seminoles. Seminoles and whites got to the point where they would even visit each other's churches in the Dania area.

Reverend Genus Crenshaw served as a Baptist missionary to the Seminoles for 49 years. During that time he was a positive influence on the Tribe until his passing in 1998. His efforts enabled former Tribal President Joe Dan Osceola to become the first Seminole to attend college. The Seminoles loved this man, and his name brings back good memories to them, though Reverend Crenshaw and other missionaries met some strong resistance from traditionalists in the Tribe and from the outside world during his tenure.

"I was invited by a Jewish attorney who at the time claimed to be working for the Indians along the Trail [Tamiami Trail], to come down and try and stop the mission work. When he called me on the phone he said I've just come from a meeting on the trail and some wanted to go out today and stop the mission work by force. He said they talked it over and decided about you, that you would get it [the effort to stop the mission work] stopped. He wanted to know if I could come down the next Sunday morning, I told him no, I'd be in church. He said what time can you come in the afternoon? I said maybe about two o'clock. So we made it to Jimmy Tiger's camp and there were a number of Indians there, maybe about twenty or more other men, women and children all around. So we talked for over two hours and they first wanted to know what the attorney told me, and I told them. Ingram Billie was a spokesman for the Indians there at that time. Tommy Tiger was the interpreter and I told him what he said. And they said, well we want you to go back to the reservation and tell those Christian Indians to have all the church preaching they want at the

Seminole Views

The Reverend Genus Crenshaw
(Photo courtesy of the *Seminole Tribune*)

reservations, but stay away from the Trail and leave us alone, we don't want it. I said well I know somebody who don't want it and I said there are some down here that do, and as long as we are invited to a camp or a public place, we'll be there. They talked it over two hours back and forth. Less than three weeks later it was published in the Miami paper that Ingram Billie had pulled out of the Trail. I later was invited to his camp to show Bible films, and shortly after he moved to Big Cypress reservation, and he and his wife became professed Christians."

—*Genus Crenshaw*

Other religious leaders are on the scene now, such as the Reverend Paul Buster (Cowbone) who is pastor of the First Seminole Indian Baptist Church. Reverend Buster has many things to deal with, such as tending to the drug and alcohol addicted, and the untimely deaths of Tribal members. Spiritual guidance of Indians who may find confusion between Christianity and old Tribal religious beliefs can be difficult. Seminoles sometimes try to hang on to old customs with one hand and Christianity with the other.

"I have made medicine for your physical needs and I did my best to do for you and help you as a medicine man, but as far as saving your souls spiritually, I cannot do that. You must do as I am doing . . . follow Jesus Christ."

—*Josie Billie,*
as told by *Cowbone (Paul Buster)*

Religious Customs

"The first were the Franciscans in the 1600s. They kept saying, in our culture that in Christianity all they ever talk about is the Son, the Father and the Holy Ghost. In our custom we don't do that; we go the mother, the father, the Son and the Holy Ghost, because we go in sequence of fours."

—James Billie

"The green papers (paper money) is God to them (some Christians). They kill to protect that piece of paper that has no life in it, but they cannot protect the God given creation, the earth and nature. We think it is just plain crazy, but yet they call themselves the Christian people."

—Bobby C. Billie

". . . At the top of the list of things that hinder Christians, people going to church and things like that is modern technology along with Seminole Tribe's business into gambling ventures and things like that.* Seminole people or Native Americans, we never really been where we are now financially. We didn't even have pennies; if we did it was just a few pennies forty years ago or even thirty years ago. But now our Seminole Tribe is pretty well affluent financially and our Seminole society does not know how to handle that — we do not know what to do with it. There are some people that are grateful and know how to invest their income, but pretty much the majority do not know what to do with it, and it's either hurting us or killing our demeanor. Some kids don't want to go to school anymore; some kids don't want to listen to their moms and dads. That's existed a long time but it's more prevalent now. When it comes to church or religion . . . nobody wants to go to church . . . no time for church. We need lots of prayers. Pray to God for his direction and guidance, raising children the way they ought to be raised, learning discipline, learning how to respect one another, to love and care for one another, whether it be different clans or whoever it may be. We need to do our best to accomplish peace in our society and to do that we must find God . . . we must know God and what He wants in our lives."

—The Reverend Paul Buster (Cowbone)

The gambling business is a large and separate subject — too large to be included in this book.

The Reverend Paul Buster (Cowbone)
(Snellings Photo)

"It is well and good to know how we Seminoles survived from the U.S. government onslaught in the early 1800's. I thank God for the courageous leaders in our Seminole history. Had it not been for their wise decisions, our existence may not be today.

"Seminoles — Native Americans — have always felt that we are different when it comes to spiritual aspects of our lives. Many of us feel that the Bible, God and the church belong to white people. But that is not true. God made everyone in this world, and He loves the whites, blacks, yellows, and yes, He also loves His Native Americans. Whether you agree or not, God loves you through His Son, Jesus.

"Jesus Christ is the Son of God. He is our Lord and Savior. God, through His Son Jesus, became a man and dwelt among us 2000 years ago. He died on the cross for my sins and your sins, that we might be saved. After the third day of His crucifixion, Jesus rose from the grave. Therefore, we have hope in Him for our souls to be saved. God loves you!!!"

—*The Reverend Paul Buster (Cowbone)*

Shortly before the turn of the nineteenth century, a Seminole choir was heard repeating the words "*Jahvey — Jahvey,*" which is the Hebrew word for God (Jehovah). It is a word forbidden by the Jews to speak because it is considered too sacred to pass from the lips of man. A Seminole man, when questioned about the word and its meaning replied, "God, white man's God." Possibly, the Seminole origin of the word *Jahvey* goes back to the Aztec temples of Mexico and the Yucatan peninsula. Maybe some of the Natives of the present day United States originated from that area of the world, thus keeping alive remnants of a

Religious Customs

culture that existed many centuries ago that were in some way touched by Christian influence or Judaism.

The Muskogee Indians are said by some to have left Mexico in the early part of the sixteenth century after Cortez conquered Mexico. These same Indians were later called "Creeks" by the British. Most historians believe that the Seminoles were originally an offshoot from the Creeks. Theoretically, some of these words (such as *Jahvey*) from the ancient cultures of which they were once a part have survived. One has but to look at today's Seminole faces to see striking resemblance to what the Aztecs are believed to have looked like and, in some cases, even to Egyptians and Israelites.

One particularly fascinating aspect of Seminole religion with some members of the Tribe is the belief that God had a Son whom He placed among the Indians His Son, named *E-shock-e-tom-issee-e-po-chee*. He was put here by God to make them "good Indians." This is, of course, a striking parallel to Christianity. In fact, the likelihood of this not stemming from Christianity at some point in time seems slim.

Seminole Views

146

Interesting Reverse Sides of Seminole Cards from the Snellings Collection.

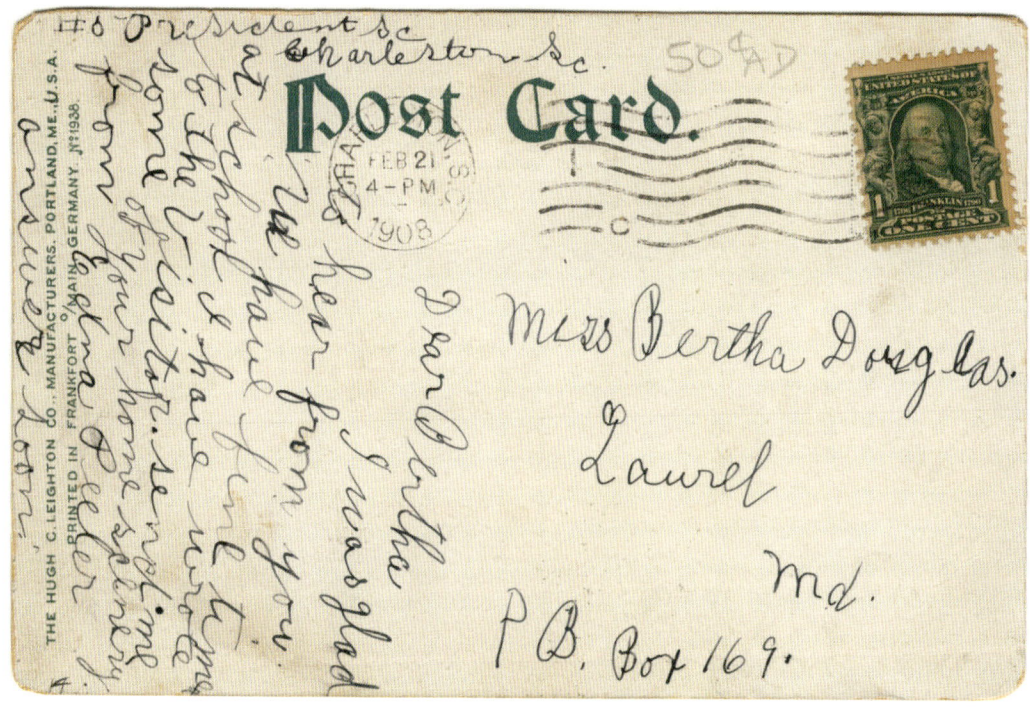

Legends

There are many legends and myths among the members of the Seminole Tribe.

Betty Mae Jumper was the first woman to become the leader of the Seminole Tribe (defeating three male opponents) and served from 1967 to 1971. In fact, she was the first female leader of any Indian tribe. During her time as chairperson, she was successful in bringing the Miccosukee, Choctaw and Cherokee into a coalition with the Seminoles called the United Southeastern Tribes. This organization now boasts a membership of over 26 tribes, and it continues to promote the welfare of Native Americans.

In 1993 Betty Mae received an honorary doctorate from Florida State University, and in 1994 she became the first Native American named to the Florida Women's Hall of Fame. Accolades are nice now, but the road there was long, hard and dangerous. The odds were against her from day one.

She is a half-breed. That was a dangerous thing to be among the Seminoles in the mid-twenties. A group of medicine men even tried to kill her when she was five years old; the only thing that saved her was her great uncle and his trusty rifle. The medicine men said she

Betty Mae Tiger
and her grandmother, Mary Gopher Tiger
(Snellings Collection)

was evil because she was only half Seminole. Betty Mae's father was a trapper who traded with the Indians, and such a situation was highly unacceptable among many members of the Tribe.

Half-breed status was also a problem when it came time to go to school. She could not go to the white school because she was part Indian; she could not go to the Black school for the same reason. A strong willed person even then, Betty Mae was determined to get an education, and finally her great uncle, Jimmy Gopher, came through for her once again. After talking with the Indian agent, he discovered that Betty Mae could go to a boarding school in Cherokee, North Carolina. So, at age 14, off she went — no longer dressed in her colorful patchwork clothing — no longer relegated to life in the chickees — no longer destined for the backbreaking life in the tomato fields where she once had worked.

"Of course my mother is an Indian Medicine Lady and she sometimes delivers a baby and she can't save it. I went to the hospital sometimes when my mother carried some people. I saw a lot of babies born in there and I think there must be some way to save them…Then was when I decided that I wanted to go to school."

—*Betty Mae Jumper*

Betty Mae became the first Seminole to finish high school and furthered her education at the Kiowa Indian Hospital in Lawton, Oklahoma, to become the first Seminole nurse. In the years following this training, she brought the white man's medicine to the Seminoles of south Florida. White man's medicine was frowned upon by the medicine men in those days,

Betty Mae and Friends

Betty Mae (Tiger, as of the date of this old postcard) loved to sing songs, and she's shown here with Mary Bowers, Agnes Denver, Charlotte Osceola (also known as Mary Tommie), and Howard Osceola. Tribal President Mitchell Cypress has undertaken the project of getting some of the old Seminole songs and hymns on tape, sung in their Native tongue. The Seminole Tribe has been blessed with excellent singers and guitar players, such as Cowbone and James Billie, and top quality flautist, Sonny Nevaquaya. (Snellings Collection)

and they believed that using it would make people sick. Betty Mae had to overcome hostile attitudes and people pointing guns at her, but gradually many of the Seminoles came to her. Thus, she began a life of service to her people for the following twenty years in the medical profession and eventually in the political arena.

In the mid-forties, romance came on the scene in Betty Mae's life. She fell in love with a Seminole alligator wrestler named Moses Jumper and they were married in 1946. Though they had two sons and a daughter and remained married for 46 years, these were turbulent times. Moses drank heavily, especially when he had flashbacks of his World War II experiences. There were times when Moses was too drunk or too sick to do his job of wrestling alligators, so Betty Mae climbed into the pit and did the job herself because her family had to be fed.

All through her life, Betty Mae has been a person of strong faith. To this day she remains steadfast in the faith that has been both an anchor and a beacon of hope throughout her life.

Seminole Views

"When I was a little girl I was taught that Christianity was the most important thing in people's lives. You learned who Jesus is and that He is who you turned to when you needed somebody the most and asked him to help you. You pray to God, and that was taught to me when I was a young girl by Willie King who was a missionary. I was raised under him and he taught me a lot of the things that I know today."

—Betty Mae Jumper

One of Betty Mae's main concerns today is the continuing education of the Seminole people without them "forgetting how to be Indian." Assimilation into America's modern cultural melting pot calls for many confusing changes on the part of Native Americans everywhere, and Betty Mae hopes that today's Seminoles can achieve this without losing their heritage. With that in mind, she wrote the book *Legends of Seminoles* (Pineapple Press). These entertaining legends taught some basic principles of life and some of the rules of behavior that apply to all human beings. Hopefully, the stories will still be told by Indian voices yet to come. The following are two Seminole legends, as told by Betty Mae:

Little People

"The older people used to tell us the Little People were in the Everglades and on the trees outside of the camp. Later on the seven dwarfs reminded me of the Little People, except there were a thousand Little People and they would all gang up and beat you. They used to scare us: 'Don't go out there by yourself or you might see the Little People!'

"When you get very sick the Little People appear at your bedside. No one but the sick person can see them. They live in the holes of the big trees. Thunder always chases and tries to kill them, but they run and disappear into the holes. This is the reason why you see lightning striking the trees. The lightning will go around and around trying to get the Little People. That is why there are so many holes in trees. The older people will always tell you never to stand under or against trees when there is lightning or you might get hit."

(Snellings Photo)

Orange Grasshoppers

"A long time ago, these grasshoppers would come out on a certain month. Every year, in the spring, millions of them would appear, everywhere. We used to play with them. I never see them any more. Not a single one.

"Many years ago, during the early part of the summer, a young orange colored grasshopper roamed the grounds everywhere. These grasshoppers would get into anything green. The people got so mad that anytime these pesky grasshoppers came around, they would be stepped on and killed.

"As the years passed, the grasshopper population lessened. Meanwhile, when people died, they would rise on the third day, and there would always be more people around to step on and kill the grasshoppers.

"The orange grasshoppers had a meeting to discuss what was happening and how soon there wouldn't be many of them left. Then one grasshopper came up with a solution: 'You all know that people rise on the third day after they die. So we must get on top of the grave, before the third day, and jump up and down on the grave so they won't come out. This will make fewer people.'

"So, to this day, when people die, they don't come up from the grave like they used to. The orange grasshoppers beat them long ago."

Seminole Views

There are many legends and myths among the members of the Seminole Tribe. Some of them are about people and some are about animals including supernatural beings of various sorts. For example, a supernatural toad in the sky called a "swallowing toad" is said to cause eclipses by swallowing the moon.

Betty Mae Jumper

(Photo courtesy of the Seminole Tribune)

The Legend of the Rabbit and the Box Turtle

One day the rabbit saw a box turtle going by in the woods and he challenged the turtle to a race. The turtle agreed to the race, but by the time of the race, he had gotten three other box turtles to help him, since there were to be four hills over which the race would go. The race finally started and the rabbit ran over the first hill and looked over to the second hill and saw the box turtle already there. The rabbit raced on to the third hill and the box turtle was there still ahead of him. By the time the rabbit got to the last hill, he was exhausted and he could see the box turtle crossing the finish line. The rabbit acknowledged his defeat and then the box turtle told him about the other three turtles who had helped him win the race. The rabbit was very upset and felt he had been cheated. The box turtle pointed out that we are all alike and that we are to help each other to solve problems in difficult times.

—by permission of the Ah-Tah-Thi-Ki Museum

"Rabbits . . . you're never supposed to eat them. If you eat it, you can catch cramps all the time . . ."

—Alice Snow

154

Seminole Views

Interesting Reverse Sides of Seminole Cards from the Snellings Collection.

Tourism

Tribal tourist attractions have helped to preserve Seminole culture.

In the early part of the twentieth century, the dredging of the Everglades and the outlawing of the plume and hide trade made it necessary for the Seminoles to find another way to survive. Thus came their involvement with the tourist trade to sell their handiwork.

The Indians in the tourist camps were generally treated well, and they received salaries and food allotments. Sometimes these businesses served as places for the members of the media to meet with Tribal leaders. Many photographs of Seminoles were taken at camps, some of which serve as valuable records of Tribal members and leaders now gone. In the thirties over half of the Seminole population was involved in some sort of tourist related business. Musa Isle and other tourist attractions of that era have helped to create an awareness of Seminole culture, which has helped to preserve it. Today the Seminoles are still heavily involved in tourism at places like Billie Swamp Safari and the Ah-Tah-Thi-Ki Museum at the Big Cypress Reservation and the Anhinga Gift Shop in Hollywood.

Musa Isle

Musa Isle was a main Seminole tourist attraction from 1910 to the forties. Attractions similar to this one were popular back in the thirties and forties and served as a place for the Seminoles to make a living selling their crafts, wrestling alligators and providing the tourists with some glimpse of Seminole life. For a 25-cent tip, tourists could have their pictures taken with Seminole families and buy a photographic postcard of that picture. Musa Isle was originally owned and managed by Willie Willie. At that time the camp was called *Oke-on-so-ho-ke-leica*, which meant "Running Water City." Willie Willie eventually lost the business to a white man, Bert Lasher, in what was considered by some to be unethical trickery. (Snellings Collection)

Trailways Card

Tourism

Transportation to Musa Isle

The boat "Jungle Queen II" seen in this old postcard is similar to the ones that carried tourists up the Miami River to visit Musa Isle and Coppinger's Pirates Cove back in the 1940's to see the Indians in their "natural surroundings." This particular boat was based in Fort Lauderdale and was advertised as having a seating capacity of 250 people. (Snellings Collection)

The Observatory in the Everglades

This early twentieth century postcard shows a viewing tower for the Everglades and the people (probably tourists) decked out in their finery for an afternoon visit to see the 'glades. Though somewhat humorous now, these visitors of old Florida saw the Everglades before development, before super highways, and before the onslaught of opportunistic politicians. (Snellings Collection)

Seminole Views

(Snellings Photo)

Billie Swamp Safari, located on the Big Cypress (*Ashawechobee*) Reservation, is a premier Seminole tourist attraction. It has traditional alligator wrestling, airboat rides, demonstrations of how the patchwork clothing is made, a reptile exhibit, swamp buggy rides, and Seminole food served at the Swamp Water Café. Occasionally there are falconry demonstrations, and Indian jewelry is sometimes sold by outside vendors. A full service gift shop is located on the premises that has postcards, jewelry, gifts made from alligator hides, Seminole clothing and a host of other items.

The Swamp Safari was opened in 1993, covers about 2,000 acres and provides the tourist with a unique opportunity to observe Seminole life (to some degree).

The Swamp Water Café serves a wide variety of foods, including frog legs, alligator, Seminole tacos, catfish and some non-Indian dishes, as well. The cooks are good and the service is friendly, with every attempt being made to make both the tourists and Tribal members feel at home.

"Seminoles did not wear big headdresses like that. This is a publicity stunt for Old South Bar-B-Q. He was a Chairman. He was a true Chief, he was Chairman from 1957–1967. That's my uncle. They used to entertain in Miss Universe contests and would greet them, Miss Universes from all over the world. And they would stop there . . . that's what it is."

—Joe Dan Osceola

According to early naturalist, William Bartram, Seminole men did decorate their bodies with vermillion paint on their heads, necks and chest. They sometimes had tattoos of animals, flowers, the sun, etc.

Chairman Billy Osceola

Seminoles were sometimes known to dress like western Indians when tourists or businesses wanted them to do so. In this card, Billy Osceola has donned his feather war bonnet for a promotional photo. (Snellings Collection)

Alligator Joe

In the early part of the twentieth century, another infamous character, Alligator Joe, would get into the pens with the gators and wrestle them for the benefit of the tourists as part of the Biscayne Navigation Company's sightseeing. (Snellings Collection)

Tourism

Alligator Farm

Alligator Joe is seen eating gator eggs while he sits at the end of a trough (possibly an old canoe) full of gator eggs. The Seminoles sometimes camped nearby on their trips to Miami from the Everglades. On one occasion, the owners of the alligator farm where Joe worked held a Christmas celebration at the Seminole camp. This event is said to be the earliest forerunner of the Seminole's involvement with alligator wrestling. (Snellings Collection)

Superman

Today the Seminole Tribe is the proud owner of "Superman," the largest gator in captivity (measuring 13 feet, 7½ inches in length), which is kept at Billie Swamp Safari on the Big Cypress Reservation. This fine crocodilian specimen gives true meaning to the James Billie's song, "*Halpatachobee,*" which means big alligator. (Snellings Collection)

Tourism

"The reason why they call him Cowboy Billy is Tex Ritter, Hoppalong Cassidy, Lash LaRue, Roy Rogers and Tom Mix. They look so good that he started dressing like them, even those arm guards. He went to extreme of being a trend setter and they named him Cowboy."

—*James Billie*

Henry Billie

Many of the Seminole alligator wrestlers were quite colorful characters such as "Cowboy Billy" (Henry Billie), shown in these cards. (Snellings Collection)

Seminole Views

The First Seminole Alligator Wrestler

Henry "Cowboy" Billie, the first Seminole alligator wrestler, poses for this group photo postcard along with others, including Henry Cypress, Tommie Bert Jumper, Holly Jumper and his family, Lilian Bowers, Cory Osceola and Elsie Jumper. (Snellings Collection)

Tom Buster

Early alligator wrestler, Tom Buster, pulls open the mouth of a big gator during a show at Musa Isle. Note the symbol in Buster's hatband. During the Second World War it was the swastika of Nazi Germany; to some Indian tribes it means peace; and, to the Seminoles it is a symbol of a man on a horse. (Snellings Collection)

Tourism

Tourism has long provided an opportunity for the Seminoles to earn money to help support (sometimes completely) their families. The peak of this activity was in the 1940s, but it still continues today with handmade crafts, such as doll-making, patchwork clothing, hand-carved figurines, novelties, art work, and others. Some of these items now bring top dollar and are even sold on the internet. There are still alligator wrestling and airboat rides along U.S. Route 41 (Tamiami Trail) and at Billie Swamp Safari on the Big Cypress Reservation. More sophisticated attractions are also available now, such as the Ah-Tah-Thi-Ki Museum, which opened in 1997 near Billie Swamp Safari. At the museum you can see artifacts, films and displays that depict tribal culture and history.

With the completion of the Hard Rock Hotels/Casinos in Hollywood, Florida, and Tampa, Florida, a myriad of shops, restaurants and activities became available to tourists who visit the Hollywood and Tampa Reservations. Powwows are held on the grounds near the casinos each year and Native vendors come from tribes all over the United States to display and sell their wares. With a yearly Tribal budget now well in excess of $100 million, more activities and special events are planned.

Alan Jumper

In this mid-twentieth century postcard Alan Jumper wrestles a big gator at Lake Charles, New York, not in Florida as the caption on the card reads. (Snellings Collection)

In recent years ecotourism has become a major activity all over Florida. In fact, it's a national trend. Since many of the Seminoles live near the Everglades or the Big Cypress Swamp, they are taking advantage of this opportunity to show people from all over the world this wilderness that is unique to south Florida.

Seminole Alligator Wrestler

In this postcard, a Seminole alligator wrestler puts an alligator "to sleep" at Musa Isle. (Snellings Collection)

14

Crafts

Crafts are not emphasized now as much as they were in the 1940s.

Crafts such as beadwork, basketry, jewelry-making and doll-making are still around today, but to a limited degree. Most of the old-timers who did this work are now gone, and the young generation of today is mostly concerned with other activities. Henry John Billie is a prime example of an old-time craftsman. He made the old hand-dugout canoes, carved wooden alligators and a host of other items; however, he is gone now, as are most other craftspeople of his time.

Handing Down the Craft

Billy Motlow teaches some young Seminoles to make little cypress canoes. Billy is gone now, but this practice of teaching children to make traditional Seminole crafts is still taught today. Crafts are not emphasized now as much as they were in mid-twentieth century; children need more than crafts to survive in today's technologically oriented world. (Snellings Collection)

Alligator Carving

This item from the author's collection, a wooden alligator carved by Henry John Billie on the Big Cypress Reservation, is an example of some of the crafts that are still alive today. Perhaps there is now even more appreciation for items such as this than there was in the tourism boom in the thirties and forties. (Snellings Photo)

Crafts

Seminole Basket

Sweetgrass baskets, such as this one owned by author Patrick D. Smith, are excellent examples of the craftsmanship and artistic abilities of the Seminoles.

A Seminole booklet reads, "They have been making sweetgrass baskets for over 60 years. Hand-picked from dry areas of the Everglades, the wild sweetgrass is washed and dried in the sun. Then it is sewn together with colored threads. Palmetto fiber is usually used to make the bases of the baskets, which are made into many different shapes."

The intricate design and beauty of these crafts make them welcome additions to many homes. (Snellings Photo)

Seminole Views

Canoe-carving
Henry John Billie carving small wooden canoes. (Snellings Collection)

Painting
Buffalo Tiger painting some of the crafts at Musa Isle. (Snellings Collection)

Crafts

Dolls

The woman depicted in this card is holding a handmade doll and her dress actually has thread sewn into this highly unusual postcard. The first accounts of doll-making were back in the late eighteen hundreds when the women made them from palmettos. Annie Tommie and Ada Tiger were two of the pioneers in this endeavor. Beautiful representations of art and manual dexterity, these dolls are highly collectible today. (Snellings Collection)

Seminole Dolls

In the beginning during the latter part of the nineteenth century, most Seminole dolls were made of just sticks and rags, but with the advent of tourism in the nineteen thirties and forties, they became more elaborate. Though reluctant at first, Seminole artisans eventually gave the dolls faces and dressed them according to Seminole dress of the day. Indians often felt that it was bad medicine to create an exact image of a person's face. The husks of palmettos were used to make the bodies of the dolls, providing appropriate hairstyles. Also, only post-menopausal women were supposed to make dolls. Today there is a doll-making competition held at the annual Seminole Tribal Fair. (Snellings Photo)

"The first doll ever made was eight inches long and they sold for fifty cents . . . It was sold at Willie Jumper's cold drink stand in front of where Howard Tommie's smoke shop is today . . ."

—Betty Mae Jumper

Crafts

173

M.146—Seminole Indian Medicine Man at Musa Isle Indian Village, Miami, Florida

Spears

Jimmy Billie is examining a spear that was made for tourists. According to his son, Bobby C. Billie, he was captured during the days of removal and taken by boat to be shipped to Oklahoma. He escaped and made his way back home to south Florida. His ancestors practiced the art of flint-napping various types of stone and coral to make magnificent spear points and arrowheads that are divided into distinct types by archeologists and other experts on Indian artifacts. The points that Jimmy's ancestors made may now have names such as Hernando, Hillsborough, Osceola-Greenbrier, Marion, Newnans, Bolen Bevel, Cypress Creek and others. If they lived in Georgia they may have had names like Savannah River, Pickwick, Little Bear Creek, Elora, Dalton, and others. The points were hafted onto shafts using sinew, gut or rawhide. The spears were sometimes thrown by hand or with the use of an atlatl. It has been centuries since any Indians in Florida used arrows and spears constructed in such a manner. (Snellings Collection)

"My father's role was that of protecting life . . . He was a good hunter."

—Bobby C. Billie, son of Jimmy Billie

Ancient Spearhead

This spearhead is probably a Putnam or a Levy style point and may be as much as 5,000 years old. This point was found in central Florida and arguably may have been made by an ancestor of some of the individuals who later became known as the Seminoles. (Snellings Photo)

Seminole Views

The Thunderbird Indian Trading Post

This Seminole trading post in Dania, Florida, no longer exists, but was active back in the forties. (Snellings Collection)

Seminole Gift Shop

Modern gift shops similar to this one are found at a variety of locations throughout the reservations. Tourists enjoy the crafts and other gifts that the Seminoles have for sale. With today's worldwide increased interest in Native American lore, sales are good. (Snellings Collection)

Children

A Seminole child's Tribal name may never be known to non-Natives.

Seminole women are very attentive to their children. This starts long before they're born.

"Even when you're pregnant, I guess non-Indian people might say it's superstition, you know how they knock on wood and all this, well, with us like when you're pregnant she (the medicine woman) tells you not to eat mangoes, the baby's navel will stick out. When the baby's born, you don't comb its hair 'til it's older, because they feel that if you comb its hair its teeth will be far apart. Or when you're pregnant you don't lean against, or like when you have a chickee, you're sitting on a platform and there's a pole, you don't lean against things and objects because that delays delivery. You don't sleep in late. You have to get up early every morning because they feel like if you lay around too much that will slow down your delivery, things like that. . . . After you have a baby and you come home, they do a whole medicine thing for you and for four months you're not allowed to eat from the same table as your family. Your child doesn't drink behind you and your husband doesn't drink behind you, you don't eat out of the same utensils, you have your own special utensils, you don't sleep with your husband for four months, you don't even sleep in the same bed with your husband, you sleep in a separate room. That's the traditional way of a pregnant woman."

—Jeanette Cypress

Jeanette Cypress with Her Grandchild

(Snellings Photo)

Children

Seminole babies are given their Indian names by an elder before they are four months old. Boys receive two names while girls receive only one. These names are not used on the birth certificate and, in fact, may never be known to non-Natives. A baby will, of course, receive an English name for legal purposes.

After four moons, babies get their first haircuts and their nails are trimmed. The trimmed locks of hair are kept by the mother. The child is then laid on white cloth and given ritual medicine to enable him or her to become a complete person. Babies may later wear bright clothes with colorful prints.

After the child is born, the mother takes a ritual bath, then she can resume marital relations when four months have passed. Traditionally (though not today), after giving birth, the new mother was from that time on to be referred to as "so and so's mother," never (or rarely) using her given name again.

> "Before they had kids they would call each other their given names, but once you have a child your child is not supposed to know your name. So then they quit calling each other by their names."
>
> —Virginia Mitchell

In past centuries a mother could kill her baby during the first month after birth if conditions for bringing up a child were unfavorable. If she did so after thirty days she would likely be treated as a murderer. This practice was abandoned long ago.

During the Seminole Wars of the nineteenth century the women had great difficulty in taking care of their children. Some parents killed their children when they thought that a child's crying would lead the soldiers to their hiding place. Holes were sometimes dug in the ground to hide the children, who were covered with palmetto fronds for protection from the sun. At night the women would carry food and water to their children.

Even the soldiers, upon capturing women and children, sometimes remarked about how badly the children had suffered. James Cook referring to the "squaws and pickaninies," said that they were an awful sight, terrified, and that their faces of the children were badly cut from running through the tall sawgrass.

Children have often been featured in Seminole postcards. The identities of so many of them are unknown today.

Seminole Indian Babies

Baby contests were some of the main events for the young children in the early to mid twentieth century. They are still held today. The child on the far right of this 1920s postcard is Laura Mae Osceola, renowned elder and advisor to the Tribe. (Snellings Collection)

Seminole Child in the Everglades

(Snellings Collection)

Nancy Osceola and Her Children

The woman in this card is wearing a good example of the old style clothing before the zigzag patterns were used. This is Nancy Osceola, wife of Josie Billie, famous medicine man of Big Cypress, with her children. (Snellings Collection)

Twin Seminole Children

Twins were considered to be evil by the Seminoles and until recent years they were sometimes killed. In the old days, such a pair as this probably would not often venture far from their home; however, the great Seminole warrior, Wildcat, had a twin sister. (Snellings Collection)

"They thought that they were evil, you only give birth to one, but when there's two there's something wrong, they used to kill them I guess. They tell us they're thunder, they're not people."

—*Mitchell Cypress*

Children

181

Posing for the Tourists

Children were often made to pose for tourists and postcard photos. Jo Jo Tiger (sling around neck), Bobby Tiger, Annie Tiger, and Louis Tiger were among those selected for this one. For the privilege of taking their picture, the children were sometimes paid a small silver coin. On some occasions tourists would simply drive by and throw a few coins at them. If a child misbehaved, he would often be switched and if he was difficult, the punishment was being scratched with needles or a snake fang. (Snellings Collection)

Seminole Views

Baby in a Shawl

A Seminole woman with her baby carried with the use of a shawl according to custom at the time is shown in this turn of the century postcard with the inscription, "Seminole Indian and Papoose." No Seminole ever referred to her baby as a papoose. Terms such as this were used by some non-Indians who knew little or nothing about Seminoles, yet felt they had to put *something* on the card. This mother and child lived around the beginning of the twentieth century and, but for this postcard, probably no record exists of their lives. (Snellings Collection)

Children

183

A Caricature

Caricatures of Indian children are sometimes used in postcards and other art work. This little girl appears to have Seminole features but she was probably not depicted as a Seminole by the artist. (Snellings Collection)

Seminole Views

Art by the Late Noah Billie

Storytellers have always been important figures in teaching children Tribal traditions, beliefs and proper ways of conduct. (Snellings Collection)

Children

185

Little John

This is an interesting little fellow wearing his vest and long shirt. His time has come and gone many years ago. None of the Tribal members that were consulted remember him. Lost to the ages, he is now known but to God. (Snellings Collection)

"He's probably got dry meat in there (the bag). We ate that a lot of that, I remember."

—Laura Mae Osceola

Seminole Views

The Willie Family

Charlie Willie, Frank Willie and family. (Snellings Collection)

Seminole Girls

Smiles adorn the faces of these happy young ladies (from left to right): Lena Johns, Augustina Gopher, and Edna Johns. Usually, the children seen in old photos displayed no smiles. (Snellings Collection)

Children

A Distant Child

Little children were often made to pose for photos and postcards when they would rather be doing something else. When they did, they might reflect the attitude of their elders, as may be the case here. Children were taught to turn their backs on white people and to reject any attempt at friendship. In fact, the women were not allowed to talk to white people or to look at them directly. (Snellings Collection)

"Seminole children were told to stay close by their mother because the white people would steal them if they didn't."

—Louise Gopher

Mother and Child at Musa Isle

(Snellings Collection)

Children Pose for a Picture

(Snellings Collection)

Enjoying Sofkee and an Alligator Ride

An old Seminole woman with a sofkee spoon and young boy on a stuffed alligator pose for a photo postcard. Again, Seminoles never referred to women as squaws or children as papooses. (Courtesy of the Miami Historical Society)

Seminole Views

Learning from Their Grandfather

George Osceola is showing his grandchildren Jenny, Billy, and Jerry some interesting pictures in a book. (Snellings Collection)

Children

Little Mr. Seminole for 1998,
Huston Osceola

(Snellings Photo)

Seminole Views

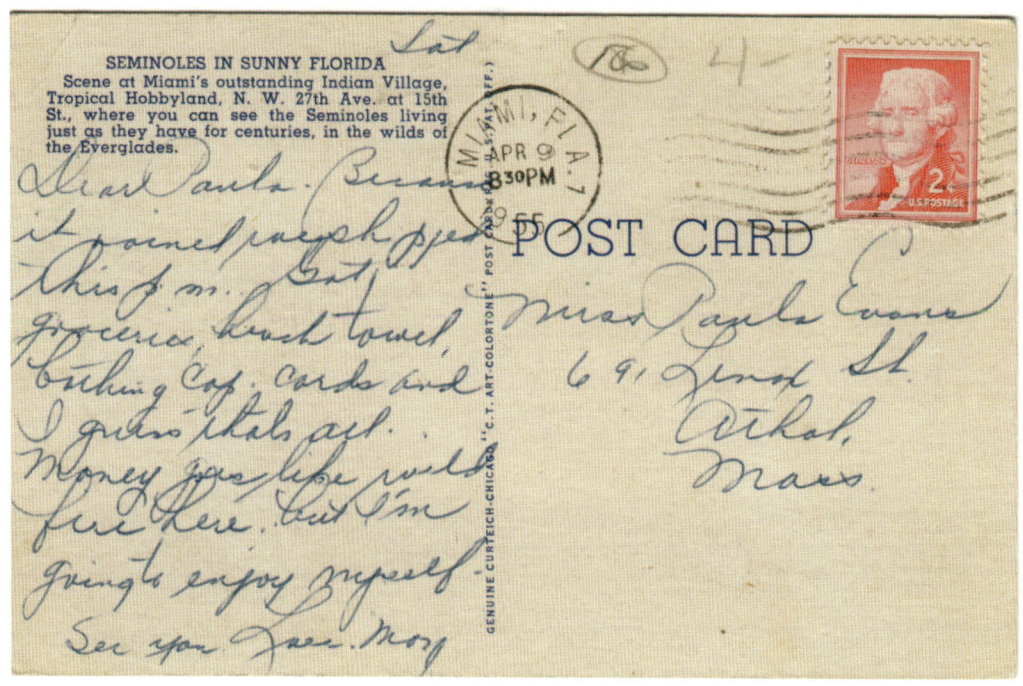

Interesting Reverse Sides of Seminole Cards from the Snellings Collection.

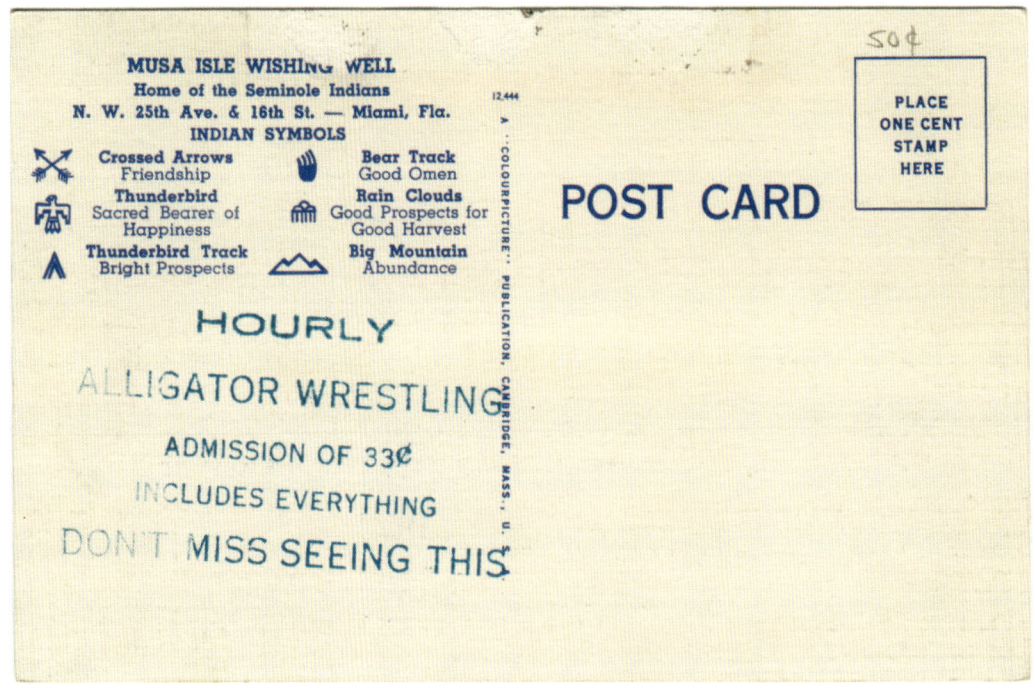

16

Education

Seminoles fear that the children will learn the modern ways and forget their Indian culture.

For a long time, the Seminoles did not want any part of the white man's education, money or help of any kind, and Indians who disagreed with this idea were punished. As the years wore on, some of the less traditional Indians began to sporadically attend makeshift schools set up by missionaries, Indian agents and Mrs. Ivy Stranahan of Fort Lauderdale, who would sometimes go to the Seminoles and teach out of her car.

Though often lumped into the broad category of "Seminole," the more traditional Seminoles and Miccosukees (sometimes called the "true" Seminoles) considered the white man's efforts to provide education to the Seminoles as a way of controlling them. Miccosukee- (Hitichi-) speaking Tribes have usually been more traditional than the Muskogee- (Creek-) speaking Seminoles. In fact, they outnumbered the Muskogee Seminoles right after the days of removal. This distinction was more apparent in the twentieth century than in the days of the Seminole Wars, when they had to stick together in their common cause of fighting the United States. Originally, the Muskogee-speaking

School Card

Elsie Jean Bowers, Richard Smith, Janette Tiger, Billy Mitchell, Coleman Josh, Brown Shoe, Eddy Shoe, and Jimmy Scott Osceola, along with a few other friends pose for the photo used in this old postcard of the Brighton Indian Day School. (Snellings Collection)

Seminoles were more agriculturally oriented, while the Miccosukee-speaking Seminoles relied more on hunting and fishing. Independent Seminoles now claim to be the most traditional, often sticking to themselves and rejecting any form of the white man's education or religion. They now reside mostly on the Tamiami Trail, near an area called "Forty Mile Bend."

The Seminoles now have schools that they run, such as Afatchkee (happy) School (K–12) on the Big Cypress Reservation and have been successful in training their students in the basic skills of elementary and secondary school education. Afatchkee School is the only elementary school in Hendry County, Florida, that is accredited by the Southern Association of Colleges and Schools. The fear among the Seminoles, and some educators, as far back as the thirties, is that the Indians will learn the modern ways and forget their Indian culture.

Efforts to "assimilate" the Seminoles into the white educational system were almost always met with stiff resistance from the old Tribal matriarchs and medicine men. Legislation like the Dawes Act of 1887 basically tried to dismantle the Indian way of life.

Education

Pioneering efforts in the twenties and thirties to educate the Seminoles in schools, to teach the white man's ways, met with little success despite the well-meaning programs and ideas of men like John Collier, James L. Glenn and Lucien A. Spencer. In fact, no effort was made to enter Seminole children into public schools until after World War II.

Going to public schools was often a hassle for Seminole children. When they finished elementary school they would sometimes have to go to high school in Clewiston, Okeechobee or Immokalee, Florida. This meant that they would have as much as a 90-mile bus ride every day — surely some sort of bussing record.

Some Seminole children went to the Cherokee Indian School during the thirties and have enjoyed successful careers. A few such as former Tribal chairman, Betty Mae Jumper (Tiger during those days), not only finished but became proficient in both the medical and political arenas. Joe Dan Osceola became the first Seminole to graduate from public high school in 1957 after attending the Okeechobee County Schools. He eventually became Tribal President and a successful businessman. Joe Dan had helped organize the Indian school at the Brighton Reservation in 1938. A list of other outstanding Tribal members would have to include Jim Shore who, despite a visual handicap, became a well-known attorney. The list of achievements of Tribal members is adding up as the resilience and adaptability of the Seminoles continue to be strong traits. It is sometimes a hard job to walk that fine line of holding on to one way of life with one hand and another way of life with the other. It can be quite confusing and frustrating to any child who tries to do this.

Prior to the educational efforts in the twentieth century, the elders of the Tribe were responsible for the transmitting of knowledge and skills to young Seminoles.

The following is taken from the book, *Stranahan House, Frank and Ivy Stranahan: New River Pioneers* by Alice Cromartie Cassels, Barbara Dinerman, Rosemary E. Jones and Stuart McIver (The Stranahan House):

Ivy Stranahan of Fort Lauderdale took great interest in the Seminole children in the 1920s and made every effort to educate them to the ways of what was then the white man's world. She faced an uphill battle with the tribal leaders, and their resistance to learning the ways of the new world in which they were going to have to survive. Nevertheless, she reached out to them with the purpose of teaching them to read and write and to introduce them to the ways of Christianity. For fifty years she spent much of her time with this goal in mind. Ivy and her husband, Frank, owned the Stranahan & Co. Trading Post on the banks of the

New River, where the Seminole often came to buy goods and sell their animal hides. There they would stay sometimes for days at a time, sleeping on the big porches that were attached to the trading post. These periodic visits provided Ivy with a wonderful opportunity to instruct the Seminole children. Upstairs in the Stranahan's quarters was a bathtub (a small one by today's standards) in which every Seminole child that came to visit had a bath. Ivy not only became well known for her educational efforts, but she also founded a group to help called The Friends of the Seminoles. "*Watchie-estra/Hutrie*" (The Little White Mother), as she was called by the Seminoles, became trusted and loved by them all.

Today, Director of Education for the Seminole Tribe, Louise Gopher, heads the now-extensive efforts to educate the Tribal members.

"My goals for the Seminole Tribe Education Program are that the language and cultural education will continue and expand to all reservations. Presently, the attention has been on the cultural staff at the Brighton Reservation who have provided cultural and language classes to their elementary students one day a week for the past three years. And in addition, they are planning to open a charter school within two years so that they can teach those classes every day to the youngsters. Programs on the other reservations have expressed interest in doing similar activities but seem to have a hard time getting it accomplished or even making attempts to provide those classes. They do have staff available that can do the teaching but haven't taken that 'step' or commitment to start the language classes. Their emphasis is more on arts and crafts and not in teaching the native language.

"I would like to see the Tribe build more charter schools or satellite schools on the reservations. Some reservations are thirty miles from town and students are traveling an hour each way to and from school. I would like to see the lower grades remain on the reservations. That way the Tribe can have some control on the curriculum and be able to include daily cultural/language classes. However, I think they should go on to schools in town at middle school and high school levels so they can experience the enrichment of being with other cultures and being part of mainstream public."

—Louise Gopher, Director of Education

Education

Professional and college athletic teams are getting a lot of criticism in recent years about the use of Native Americans as mascots or logos. Critics claim that such mascots are dehumanizing and show disrespect for the person or people depicted in the logo. Feelings differ among the various Tribes across the country, but most Seminoles are very much in favor of their association with Florida State University. Osceola is now considered to be their official mascot. This university was defended on one occasion by a Tribal official who rebutted a proposed idea that the Tribe should be compensated for the use of the name Seminole.

FSU Card
(Snellings Collection)

"We have a very good working relationship with Florida State University, they roll out the red carpet for our students that go there, they give them an A-1 education, it is a very, very highly established learning institute. For them to treat our young Seminoles in the fashion in which they do is payment enough. We could receive monetary gains for someone using our name, but the education that is bestowed upon our children is something that money could never buy, something that could never be taken away from them. By doing that they are assisting the Tribe for the future, preparing us for what is yet to come that we have not dreamed. We may receive monetary gains today when it could be spent tomorrow or the next month or next year, but knowledge is the key to all success. Some of our people gain that knowledge from Florida State University. Their facility has decided to call themselves Seminoles. Why, because we are just that, the strong, the brave, the Seminole, and they want to be tagged with us. We know who we are. We don't need a group of people to tell us who we are. We know where we come from, we then know where we're going, so why should we have opposition to someone that is doing us a good service for our future, not just for today."

—Sally Tommie

Though most people believe that education and technology are necessary for humans to survive in today's complicated world and to maintain a good quality of life, not all Seminoles agree.

"Because of so-called technology one person can destroy thousands of acres a day. The newcomer's mind is off and running without thinking. You need to stop. Because I am Indigenous Person, I'm speaking to you because you have the right to protect your future generation yet to come. What are they going to have after all of nature is gone? Your elders are going to leave you this problem. You need to wake up now and do something. You need to cut down your population. You're growing like a cancer — a cancer on the body killing a person. Sometimes the truth can hurt, but the truth needs to be spoken."

—Bobby C. Billie

17

Cattle Business

In South Florida, the Indians might be the real cowboys.

By 1750 the Seminole, with the help of the white man's long guns, had greatly depleted the deer herds. They began to raise cattle, rounding up the wild cattle that the Spanish had abandoned. Herds were privately owned and became a status symbol of sorts. The land, however, belonged to everybody. Private property was an alien notion to Native Americans at that time.

Two centuries later, things had greatly changed. The Tribe had been almost destroyed by both the warfare with the United States in the nineteenth century and the subsequent removal tactics. The few Seminoles left to survive in the 'glades had survived mostly on hunting and fishing until drainage and the onslaught of humanity from the North sort of pigeonholed many of them into making a living in the tourist business. Through all this, many of the Seminoles have always been interested in raising cattle; so, when efforts began to "assimilate" the Indians into the white man's economic structure of the twentieth century, state and federal agencies did begin to offer some help.

Seminole Views

A True Cowboy

Paul Bowers of the Big Cypress Reservation gettin' ready to ride before rodeo time. (Snellings Photo)

The United States government purchased and shipped about 500 head of Hereford cattle to the Seminole Indian Agency in 1936. The cattle arrived in poor condition; some of them were dead when they arrived. Many of the living cattle died on the drive to the reservation. But the Tribe made the best of the situation and operated the animals as a government herd until 1938, when the Tribe was persuaded to take over. With the help of the Extension Service of the United States, they were successfully into a well-established enterprise. The Seminoles purchased a significant amount of cattle from the Apache Reservation in Arizona, with the United States government advancing the money. The Seminoles continued to develop the herd until the proceeds of the cattle business paid back the government.

Tribal herds were placed on both the Brighton and the Big Cypress Reservations and these herds were eventually dispersed into individual ownership in 1954. Each reservation formed its own cooperative association, and the cattle business was thriving. As far back as 1962, the Seminoles had over 6,000 head of cattle. Today business is booming; they now have over 15,000 head of cattle on the Big Cypress Reservation alone. There are even big Seminole rodeos. The cattle business is one of the most successful business enterprises that the Seminoles have undertaken. It looks like that here, in South Florida, the Indians might be the real cowboys.

Along with the cattle business is a booming citrus business for the Seminoles. On the Big Cypress Reservation there are wide varieties of citrus crops: Hamlin and Valencia oranges, Flame Red, Ray Red and White Marsh grapefruit, Mucott mandarin oranges, Robinson tangerines, Orlando tangeloes, and the largest crop of lemons in the United States, involving some 10,000 acres. There is also a large crop of bell peppers covering about 1,000 acres of land.

Florida's Seminoles now hold controlling interest in one of the major herds of Red Brahma in the United States. A vigorous breed of cattle, the Red Brahmas are strong and withstand harsh climates. These animals secrete a substance called sebum from their skin that is oily and repels tenacious Florida insects. Healthy and productive for many years, the Red Brahman cattle provide a source of lean beef that is quite desirable on today's market.

"We've got about eighteen thousand acres of improved pastures, we figure three acres per cow on improved pastures and about thirty acres for unimproved. We have thirty-four thousand acres more or less and we use most of it right now. We have forty-three individual operators that constitute the cattle program, and each person has to sign a release with the Tribe saying that they will be in this program for the next ten years. They are all color coded, so each person has their own areas that we keep them in. We control breed so that all calves fall at the same time, hopefully."

—*Stanlo Johns*

(These figures were as of 1999 and may have changed slightly as of this printing.)

A Brahma Bull

As of the turn of the twenty-first century, the Seminoles have over 15,000 head of cattle on the Big Cypress Reservation alone. (Snellings Collection)

Moving Cattle

As though it were a scene from Patrick D. Smith's book, *A Land Remembered*, this cowboy moves these head of cattle along through the palmettos. In the early days of the Seminoles, back when Cowkeeper was their leader, they tended large numbers of cattle similar to the ones depicted in this postcard. The Seminoles were doing this long before anybody ever heard the words "Florida Cracker." (Snellings Collection)

18

All Things Seminole

Florida abounds with Seminole names.

Seminole names persist throughout modern Florida history to denote a wide variety of things. *Okeechobee* (Lake Okeechobee) means big water. *Allapattah* (a Seminole novel by Patrick Smith), from the Seminole word *halpatee*, means alligator. *Oklawaha* (Oklawaha River) means boggy. *Tallahassee*, Florida's capitol city, is named after a band of Seminoles that once inhabited that area. *Alachua* (Alachua County) was the name of a band of Seminoles that once inhabited the Payne's Prairie region of northern Florida. *Hatchineha* (Lake Hatchineha) means cypress tree. *Wekiva* (Wekiva River — sometimes called Wekiwa) means spring. *Apopka* (Lake Apopka and the town of Apopka) means potato-eating place. *Bithlo* (the town of Bithlo) means dugout canoe. The name Seminole itself denotes both a city and a county in Florida, a highway in Virginia, a mascot for Florida State University, a railroad line, and a name for countless clubs, developments and shopping centers. The list is almost endless and proves the historical influence that this small Tribe has had on the Southeast and the state of Florida in particular.

The Seminole Club in Miami

Clubs bearing the Seminole name were around, even at the turn of the century like this one in Miami, Florida. (Snellings Collection)

All Things Seminole

Tiger Family Children

The exact date that the photo for this postcard was taken is unknown, but is prior to 1907 because there is no dividing line down the middle of the back of the card. Most of the children in the card are of the Tiger family including Tommy, Bobby, Jo Jo, Micky, Tiger and Buffalo. (Snellings Collection)

The last name Tiger probably comes from the early white settlers who mislabeled the Florida panther as a tiger. White traders and store owners often bestowed such names on Seminoles because they couldn't pronounce or didn't know their Indian names or because they wanted to make some sort of sick joke. In other cases the Indian surname was used for the last name (Jack Tigertail, Charlie Cypress, etc.). Yet others may bear the name of a Tribal hero (John Osceola, Alan Jumper, etc.). Osceola is a prominent name among the Seminoles, but because of the constant mispronunciation of the name by non-Natives, the Indians began using this incorrect spelling of the name "Asiyaholo." In fact, the name "Seminole" is not liked by some Tribal members — it's simply tolerated. A century ago the Seminoles who were removed to Oklahoma referred to the Florida Seminoles as *Ikanyuksalgi*, meaning "people of the peninsula."

Shirt-Tail Charlie and Sam Huff

This postcard shows Shirt-tail Charlie and Sam Huff. (Snellings Collection)

Shirt-Tail Charlie

Shirt-tail Charlie was one of the most infamous members of the Seminole Tribe. An alcoholic, Charlie panhandled the streets of Fort Lauderdale on the New River near what is now Eighth Avenue and Broward Boulevard during the early 1920s. He rarely bathed, and when he did it was considered by the locals to be a monumental event.

There is a legend about Charlie that tends to vary, depending upon who tells it. He is said to have murdered his wife and, thus, was banned from the Tribe and that he was henceforth required to wear only a one piece "longshirt" as part of this punishment. (It was actually a Seminole warrior's hunting shirt made of calico.) He lived totally alone. It is said that he was quite athletic in his time and that he captured seven alligators with his bare hands during a single hunt.

Charlie did not kill his wife. Mrs. Frank Stranahan buried Charlie's wife, and she claimed that the woman died of natural causes. This brings one to question the whole validity of the story. He may have been simply a drunken outcast; but, he was nevertheless a colorful character. Shirt-tail Charlie died sometime around 1930 in a drunken stupor with his face buried in a puddle of mud. He was buried near the Seaboard Coastline Railroad track near where he spent much of his time. Tony Tommie helped bury him with all of his worldly possessions — a knife, a metal pot and his shirt.

Today a fine seafood restaurant exists on the New River called Shirt-tail Charlie's. It overlooks the river where the old "Jungle Queen" boats used to travel, now replaced by newer ones. A picture of disheveled Charlie, sitting cross-legged and holding a tarpon, hangs on a wall inside. There you can sit, enjoy the great food, sip on a drink and imagine what it was like back in Charlie's day.

State Seal Cards

Both a Seminole man and a Seminole woman have been featured on the Florida state seal. The lower card, as the map shows, was printed long before all the interstate highways. (Snellings Collection)

State Seal Cards

(Snellings Collection)

All Things Seminole

Re-enactors Samuel Tommie and Cathy Jumper

These modern Seminoles re-enact various scenes for the Ah-Tah-Thi-Ki Museum, and they play important roles in the introductory film at the museum. (Courtesy of the Ah-Tah-Thi-Ki Museum)

The Ah-Tah-Thi-Ki Museum

Anyone visiting the museum will want to be sure to see the introductory video and to visit the gift shop where there are many Seminole arts and crafts for sale. (Courtesy of the Ah-Tah-Thi-Ki Museum)

Seminole Views

On August 21, 1997, the Seminole Tribe of Florida celebrated the grand opening of the Ah-Tah-Thi-Ki Museum. Combined with the efforts of the National Museum of the American Indian, the Tribe has worked to develop a place where everyone interested in the history of the Tribe can come to see artifacts and to study the various aspects of Seminole life. Housed in a modern building on the Big Cypress Reservation, the museum has documented over 400 artifacts, which include many examples of clothing, jewelry, musical instruments, dolls, baskets, cooking utensils and enlargements of old photographs for people to see. The boardwalk outside the museum gives the visitor an opportunity to walk through a swamp typical of the life-sustaining environments that early Seminoles called home. Along this walkway are signs that explain some of the plants to be seen and an explanation of their medicinal uses.

The museum provides a unique opportunity for Tribal members to learn about their history. Now is the time to preserve the history, folklore and culture of the Seminole Tribe or risk losing valuable artifacts and information forever. With the opening of this center for learning, the Seminole Tribe of Florida is once again taking a leading role in the preservation of Native American history.

> "This country (Florida) was made for the Seminoles and they should be permitted to live here undisturbed forever."
>
> —Grover Cleveland, President of the United States

The Seminoles are no different than other groups, races, and nations in that they have differing factions with their own ideas of the way things should be done. Powerful personalities exist in each of these groups — The Seminole Tribe of Florida, The Miccosukee Tribe of Indians of Florida, and the Independent Traditional Seminole Nation of Florida. Each of the leaders among these Tribes has much to contribute to the retention of the history and culture of the Indians of South Florida. Altogether they may number over 4,000 people as of this writing. If all of these Tribal leaders and members could come together and work toward the common cause of preserving their culture, while at the same time moving forward in a world they cannot escape, their strength would increase. These are a people not without vision and purpose, yet their position is not as strong as it could be. Historically, those who can adapt to situations they are unable to change are the ones who survive. Seminoles must examine ideas that may be new to them. Even the oldest of traditions was once new. This doesn't mean to forget the old ways or the ancestors of yesteryear; it does mean that the opportunities now provided in this nation that once persecuted the Indians must be used to their full advantage. The most powerful voice with which to do that would be a united voice in which no one would doubt their resolve. Together they can make sure that Seminole blood endures as long as the waters flow.

Che-he-cha-lah. "See you later."

(There is no word for goodbye in Mikosuki [Miccosukee].)

References

A

Arndorfer, Bob. 2000. "Canoeing Down History." Gainesville: *Gainesville Sun*.

B

Bean, Tommy. 2001. "Texas Brahmans Bound for B. C." Hollywood: *Seminole Tribune*.

Blake, Libby. 2000. "A Moment in Time." Hollywood: *Seminole Tribune*.

Bucuvalas, Tina, Peggy A. Bulger and Stetson Kennedy. 1994. *South Florida Folklife.* Jackson: University of Mississippi Press.

Buker, George E. 1975. *Swamp Sailors.* Gainesville: University Press of Florida.

C

Capron, Louis. 1956. "Florida's Wild Indians. The Seminole." *National Geographic.* Washington, DC: National Geographic Society.

Cory, C. B. 1895. *Hunting and Fishing in Florida.* Boston: Barta Press.

Covington, James W. 1993. *The Seminoles of Florida.* Gainesville: University Press of Florida.

———. 1968. "Migration of the Seminoles Into Florida, 1700–1820." *Florida Historical Quarterly.* Jacksonville: Florida Historical Society.

Crute, Joseph H. Jr. .1987. *Units of the Confederate States Army.* Gaithersville: Old Soldier Books, Inc.

D

Densmore, Frances. 1956. *Seminole Music.* (United States Bureau of American Ethnology Bulletin 161.) DeCapo, Publisher.

Downs, Dorothy. 1995. *The Art of the Florida Seminole and Miccosukee Indians.* Gainesville: University Press of Florida.

F

Federal Writer's Project of the Work Projects Administration for the State of Florida. 1940. *Florida, A Guide to the Southernmost State.* New York: Oxford University Press.

Flowers, Charles. 2000. "Federal Protection Sought for Newnan's Lake." Hollywood: *Seminole Tribune*.

G

Giddings, Joshua R. 1858. *Exiles of Florida.* Columbus: Follette, Foster & Company.

Glen, James Lafayette. 1982. *My Work Among the Seminoles.* Gainesville: University Press of Florida.

J

James, Michael. 2000. "Okeechobee Battle Site: Save It or Lose It Forever." Hollywood: *Seminole Tribune*.

Johnson, Sandy. 1994. *The Book of the Elders.* New York: Harper Collins.

Johoda, Gloria. 1975. *The Trail of Tears.* New York: Wing Books.

Josephy, Alvin M., Jr. 1994. *500 Nations*. New York: Alfred A. Knopf.

K

Kersey, Harry A., Jr. 1985. *The Florida Seminoles and the New Deal 1933-1942*. Boca Raton: Florida Atlantic University Press.

———. 1973. "Pelts, Plumes and Hides: White Traders Among the Seminole Indians, 1890-1930." Tampa: *Florida Historical Quarterly*, January, 1973, Florida Historical Society.

———. 1970. "Educating the Seminole Indians of Florida." Tampa: *Florida Historical Quarterly*, July, 1970, Florida Historical Society.

L

Ledere, Vida. 2001. "Charlie Tigertail: Early Trader Helped Everyone." Hollywood: *Seminole Tribune*.

M

MacCauley, Clay. 1887. *The Seminole Indians of Florida*. Washington, DC: Smithsonian. (Book Reprint 2000. Gainsville: University Press of Florida.)

Mahan, John K. 1967. *History of the Second Seminole War.* Gainesville: University Press of Florida.

Mathiessen, Peter. 1984. *Indian Country*. New York: Penguin Books.

McCarthy, Kevin M. 1999. *Native Americans in Florida*. Sarasota: Pineapple Press.

McCoy, Kim. 2002. "Indian Group Small But Active." Greenville: *The Greenville News*.

McEwan, Bonnie G. 2000. *Indians of the Southeast*. Gainesville: University Press of Florida.

McIver, Stuart. 1989. *True Tales of the Everglades*. Miami: Florida Flair Books.

McReynolds, Edwin C. 1972. *The Seminoles*. Norman: University of Oklahoma Press.

Meltzer, Milton. 1972. *Hunted Like a Wolf.* New York: Garrar, Straus and Giroux.

Miller, Susan A. 2003. *Coacoochee Bones*. Lawrence: University Press of Kansas.

Milne, Courtney. 1995. *Sacred Places in North America: a journey into the medicine wheel.* New York: Stewart, Tabori & Chang.

Mitchell, Virginia. 2000. "The Good Old Ways." Hollywood: *Seminole Tribune*.

N

Nabokov, Peter. 1991. *Native American Testimony*. New York: Penguin Books.

Neil, Wilfred T. 1956. *Florida's Seminole Indians*. St. Petersburg: Great Outdoors Publishing Co.

O

Overstreet, Robert M. 2001. *Indian Arrowheads*. New York: Gemstone Publishing, Inc.; The Crown Publishing Group.

S

Seminole Wars Historic Foundation, Inc. "A Legacy of Courage 1817–1858." Dade City: Historical Foundation, Inc.

Sturtevant, William Curtis. 1955. "The Mikasuki Seminole: Medical Beliefs and Practices." Yale University: Doctoral Dissertation.

T

"The 40th Anniversary of the Seminole Tribe of Florida - Grand Opening of Ah-Tha-Thi-Ki Museum." 1997. Hollywood: Seminole Communications; *Seminole Tribune*.

V

Volkert, Vida. 1999. "Ft. Dallas Provided a Base for a Whole New Type of Warfare." Hollywood: *Seminole Tribune*.

W

Wall, Steve and Harvey Arden. 1990. *Wisdom Keepers*. Hillsboro: Beyond Words Publishing Company.

Weisman, Brent Richards 1999. *Unconquered People: Florida's Seminole and Miccosukee Indians.* Gainesville: University Press of Florida.

West, Patsy. 2002. *The Seminole and Miccosukee Tribes of Southern Florida*. Charleston: Arcadia Publishing Co.

———. 1998. *The Enduring Seminoles*. Gainesville: University Press of Florida.

———. 1996. "I.Laponki. The Florida Seminoles in the 1930s." Phoenix: Native Peoples.

Wickman, Pat. 2000. "Pithlachocco's Canoes: Nature's Millennium." Hollywood: *Seminole Tribune*.

———. 1999. "Seminole Colors." Hollywood: Seminole Publications — Seminole Tribe of Florida.

———. 1999. *The Tree That Bends*. Montgomery: University of Alabama Press.

Wilson, Minnie Moore. 1911. *The Seminoles of Florida.* New York: Moffat, Yard & Co.

Y

Yari, Ethel. 1999. "James Billie, Seminole Chief, Leads His Tribe Into the 21st Century." Lakeland. *Florida Living.*

Permissions

B

Bobby C. Billie — culture, environmental issues, gravesite concerns, photo

Henry John Billie — the building of hand dugout canoes, crafts, photo

James Billie — religion, Florida panther, writers

Susie Jim Billie — culture, photo

Paul Bowers — Naha Tiger, photo

Paul Buster (Cowbone) — religion, culture, legend

C

Billy Cypress — language, Ingram Billie

Jeanette Cypress — culture, history, women's interests, photo

Mitchell Cypress — concern for the Everglades, twins, photo

Genus Crenshaw — story about Josie Billie

D

Pat Diamond — gopher story, photo, general interview

G

Lorene Gopher — general interview

Louise Gopher — culture, education

H

Bobby Henry — rainmaking, photo, canoe-making

J

Annie Jimmie — culture, photo

Stanlo Johns — cattle

Betty Mae Jumper — culture, dolls, legends, religion

Moses Jumper — poem, sofkee information

L

Guy LeBree, painting

M

Mary Martin Ltd. — for section about postcards

Christine E. McCall — photo

Virginia Mitchell — culture

N

Jo North — general interview

O

Jimmy O'Toole Osceola — general interview

Joe Dan Osceola — culture, gift shop, education

Laura Mae Osceola — culture, photo

William Osceola — photo only

Swamp Owl (Virgil P. Morrison II) — general interview and photo

R

Larry Roberts — postcard business

S

Geneva Shore — the Polly Parker story (a Xerox copy that she made for use in the book). This copy was obtained in the Seminole Genealogy Department

Mary Jane Storm — general interview

T

Buffalo Tiger — culture, environmental concerns, photo

Danny Tommie — environmental concerns

Sally Tommie — her grandmother's stories, FSU, photo

P

Pineapple Press, Inc. — cited at the front of the book

S

Seminole Tribe of Florida and Tribal Council — cited at the front of the book

Index

A

A Land Remembered, 105 (*see also* Smith, Patrick D.)
Ah-Tah-Thi-Ki Museum, 25, 29, 44, 66, 72, 80, 87, 95, 136, 153, 155, 165, 209, 210
Allapattah, 203 (*see also* Smith, Patrick D.)
Alligator, 12–13, 51 (*see also* Halpatter Tustenuggee)
Alligator Alley, 127
alligator boats, 16
alligators, 16, 41, 65, 77, 106, 111, 140, 158, 160–62, 164–65, 189, 203, 206
ancestors, 3, 95, 125, 139, 173, 210 (*see also* artifacts)
Anhinga Gift Shop, 34, 155
animal hides, 27, 77, 79-80, 89-90, 94, 96, 106, 116, 131, 133, 135, 148, 155, 158, 196
art, 95, 101, 120, 165, 171, 183-84, 196, 209
artifacts, 93, 125, 165, 173, 210 (*see also* ancestors)
Asanyole, 50
Ashawechobee, 158 (*see also* Big Cypress)
Ashley, John, 27
Asiyahola!, 134 (*see also* Asiyaholo)
Asiyaholo, 50, 205 (*see also* Osceola)
assimilation, 194 (*see also* Dawes Act)
Aviaka (Abiaki, Avaika, Apeika), 11, 13, 18, 52 (*see also* Jones, Sam)

B

babies, 13, 122, 148, 175, 177–78, 182 (*see also* children)
Bartram, William, 5–6, 79, 137, 159 (*see also* Puc Puggy)
battles, 22, 43 (*see also* wars)
　Battle of Cabin Creek, 20
　Battle of Okeechobee, 11, 13, 15
　Battle of Withlacoochee, 12
beads, 69, 70, 79, 80, 81, 82, 83, 86, 87, 96 (*see also* jewelry)
bears, 14, 106, 115
Bedell, Deaconess, 81, 139–41
beliefs, 140, 184 (*see also* God *and* religion)
beverages
　black drink, 50, 134
　sofkee, 65–66, 68, 76, 126, 127, 189
　See also food.
Bible, The, 55, 96, 135, 140, 142, 144
Big Cypress, 25
Big Cypress Preserve, 117, 119
Big Cypress Swamp, 1, 165
Billie, 77, 135
　Addie, 4
　Alice, 4
　Annie, 89
　Bobby C., 18, 24, 39, 43, 84, 110, 112, 113, 117, 139, 143, 173, 198
　Chestnut, 63, 98
　Concho, 4
　Frank, 28, 38
　Henry, 163, 164 (*see also* Billy, Cowboy)
　Henry John, 94, 95, 100, 167, 168, 170
　Ingram, 28–29, 46, 127, 131, 141–42
　James, 25, 28, 37, 57, 69, 116, 130, 132, 137, 143, 149, 162, 163
　Jimmie, 28
　Jimmy, 39, 173
　Josie, 25, 28, 39, 46, 126, 131, 142, 179
　Lena Osceola, 89
　Little, 28
　Louise, 66, 86
　Mary, 66
　Miami, 4
　Mona, 75

Billie, continued
  Mona Tiger, 63
  Mr., 95
  Noah, 17, 67, 120, 184
  Rosie, 80
  Ruby, 28, 88
  Sallie, 80, 82
  Sonny, 19, 123
  Suzie Jim, 70, 75, 124, 125
  Tom, 109
  Tom "Homespun", 123
Billien, Charlie 63
Billy, Cowboy, 163 (*see also* Billie, Henry)
birds, 29, 44, 52, 75, 77, 80–81, 107, 133–35, 137–38
Biscayne Navigation Company, 160
Black Seminoles, 55–58, 137 (*see also* Blacks)
Blacks, 5, 7, 9, 12, 50, 55–57, 126, 137, 148 (*see also* Black Seminoles *and* slaves)
Bok Tower, 57
Bowers,
  Elsie Jean, 194
  Lilian, 164
  Mary, 149
  Paul, 26
Bowlegs,
  Billy, 13, 16, 30, 32 (*see also* Holata Micco)
  Billy, III, 26, 31
Breathgiver, 129, 137 (*see also* Breathmaker; Creator; *and* God)
Breathmaker, 25 (*see also* Breathgiver; Creator; *and* God)
Bright, James B., 62
Brighton Indian Day School, 194
Buster,
  Johnny, 28
  Maggie Billie, 75, 89
  The Reverend Paul, 76, 142, 144 (*see also* Cowbone)
  Tom, 164

C

camps, 1, 4, 6, 57, 60, 62–64, 69, 74–75, 85, 131, 136, 139, 140–42, 150, 155–56,
  Chestnut Billie's Camp, 63, 74–75
  Cuscowilla, 6
  Jimmy Tiger's Camp, 141
  Pirate's Cove Camp, 45

canals, 99, 110, 113
canoes, 12, 13, 27, 33, 73, 77, 90, 93–96, 97, 98, 99, 100, 101, 106, 112, 139, 161, 167, 170, 203
Cassels, Alice Cromartie, 195
Castro, Fidel, 40
Catlin, George, 51
cattle, 6, 7, 14, 22, 26, 106 (*see also* Tribal business, cattle)
Cavillo, John, 55
celebrations, 130, 135
  Celebrate Native America Day, 20
  Christmas, 19, 161
  See also Green Corn Dance.
ceremonies
  burials, 25, 137–39
  purification ceremony, 134
  Tribal, 130
  weddings, 37 49, 56, 135–37, 142
  See also death.
Chakika, 99
chants, 121, 123, 127, 131 (*see* also songs)
Chechoter, 50 (*see also* Morning Dew)
chickees, 1, 6, 59–62, 64, 67–69, 76, 148, 175 (*see also* chigets)
chiefs, 40, 46, 49, 51, 55, 57, 159 (*see also* leaders)
chigets, 59 (*see also* chickees)
children, 13–14, 32, 36, 47, 61, 68, 74, 96, 106, 122, 125, 127, 134–35, 141, 143, 175–92, 193, 195–97, 205 (*see also* babies)
Chipco, 57
Christianity, 24–25, 96, 129, 139, 141–43, 145, 150, 195 (*see also* Jesus)
churches, 37, 139, 141–44
cimarrones, 5
cities
  Florida
    Alachua, 203
    Apopka, 203
    Bithlo, 203
    Brighton, 26, 41, 62
    Bushnell, 11, 50
    Chokoloskee, 77, 85
    Clewiston, 195
    Dania, 45, 62, 96, 141, 174
    Everglades City, 11, 139
    Fort Lauderdale, 19, 45–46, 95, 100, 109, 157, 165, 193, 195, 206
    Gainesville, 60
    Hollywood, 34, 41, 60, 62, 155
    Immokalee, 62, 69, 195
    Jacksonville, 60
    Key West, 60
    Lakeland, 24
    Lake Wales, 57
    Miami, 19, 40, 45, 57, 62, 85, 111, 140, 142, 161, 204
    Miccosukee, 5
    Naples, 42, 48
    New Smyrna, 134
    Ochopee, 127
    Okeechobee, 34, 195, 203
    Oklawaha, 203
    Pensacola, 19, 60
    Picolata, 6
    Pine Island, 109
    St. Augustine, 3, 53
    St. Marks, 19
    St. Petersburg, 20
    Sanford, 112
    Tallahassee, 5, 57, 203
    Tampa, 11–12, 19, 62, 126, 165
    Tequesta, 3
  Georgia
    Fowltown, 10
  Louisiana
    New Orleans, 33
  New York
    Lake Charles, 165
  North Carolina
    Cherokee, 148
  Oklahoma
    Lawton, 148
  South Carolnina
    Charleston, 14, 53
Civilian Conservation Corps, 106
clans, 24, 47, 52, 63, 68, 107, 130–31, 134, 136–37, 143
  Alligator Clan, 137
  Big Blue Heron Clan, 107
  Big Town Clan, 137
  Bird Clan, 131, 137
  Deer Clan, 137
  Otter Clan, 68, 137
  Panther Clan, 28, 131
  Snake Clan, 137
  Wind Clan, 68, 131
Clay, Ruby Billie, 75
clothing, 31, 58, 77, 79–91, 94, 137–38, 140–41, 210

clothing, continued
  hats, 17, 31, 58, 80, 87, 91, 138
  blouses, 80
  breechcloths, 17, 79–80
  pouches, 133
  capes, 66, 80
  contests, 85
  scarves, 30
  dresses, 80, 90
  jackets, 30, 34–35, 79–81, 90
  kerchiefs, 17, 57
  leggings, 80
  moccasins, 17, 79
  old style, 89, 179
  patchwork, 24, 77, 79, 80-82, 84, 86, 88, 148, 158, 165, 177, 179
  shawls, 182
  shirts, 17, 77, 79, 80, 138, 185
  skirts, 69–70, 80
  Spanish moss for, 86
  vests, 58, 80, 90, 185
Cloud, Major George, 20
Coacoochee, 12, 14, 52 (*see also* Wildcat)
colleges, 20, 141 (*see also* universities)
Collier, John, 62, 195
Conapatchie, Billie, 24
concentration camps, 33
Confederate Army, 20 (*see also* wars, Civil War)
Cook, James, 177
cooking equipment, 65, 74, 210 (*see also* fires *and* kitchens)
Cootihattie, 34 (*see also* Osceola, Joe Dan)
Cortez, 145
Cory, C. B., 138
court day, 133–34
Cowbone, 25, 76, 118, 142–44, 149 (*see also* Buster, The Reverend Paul)
Cowkeeper, 5, 6, 7, 122, 137
crafts, 62, 96, 140, 155–56, 165, 167–74, 196, 209
  basketry, 167, 169, 210
  carving, 165, 167–68, 170
  doll-making, 76, 165, 167, 171–72, 210
  See also clothing, patchwork.
Creator, the, 43, 107, 110, 115, 130, 133, 139 (*see also* Breathgiver *and* God)

Crenshaw, The Reverend Genus, 141–42
crimes, 24, 68, 130, 134, 136 (*see also* punishments)
Crop-eared Charlie, 134 (*see also* Tiger, Charlie)
Cuba, 5, 29, 40–41
culture, 78, 85, 125, 133, 135, 141, 145, 155, 165, 193–94, 196, 210 (*see also* traditions)
cypress wood, 59, 94–95, 97, 104, 116, 119, 203 (*see also* cypress canoes *and* trees)
Cypress,
  Billy, 23, 28, 88, 133
  Charlie, 97, 205
  Henry, 48, 164
  Jeanette, 122, 124, 176
  Johnny, 38
  Mitchell, 21, 33, 149, 180
  Roy, 99
  Wilson, 140

D
Dade, Major Francis L., 11–12, 50, 56
Dallas, Navy Commander Alexander, 19
dances, 130, 135, 140
  alligator dance, 131
  ancient old festival dance, 130
  catfish dance, 131
  chicken dance, 131
  corn dances, 135
  hunting dance, 131
  rain dance, 126–27
  screech owl dance, 131
dance circle, 131
Dawes Act, 194 (*see also* assimilation)
day of fasting, 131
de Leon, Ponce, 3
death, 129, 137–38, 142, 151 (*see also* ceremonies, burials)
deer, 68, 77, 80, 106, 108, 131, 133
Denver, Agnes, 149
depression, the, 106, 121
development, 112, 157
Devil's Garden, 11
Diamond, Pat, 69–71
dikes, 111
Dinerman, Barbara, 195
directions, 133, 135, 138
discipline, 143 (*see also* punishment)

diseases, 18, 32, 129, 150
  alcoholism, 24, 55, 105, 127, 134, 142, 149, 206
  dysentery, 33
  heart disease, 74
  high blood pressure, 74, 121
  infections, 127
  malaria, 33, 53, 126
  pyorrhea, 127
  tuberculosis, 127
  See also sicknesses.
Disston, Hamilton, 110
Doctor,
  Doctor, 108
  John, 108
  Tommy, 24
dogs, 25, 29, 94, 137
dreams, 126, 129
dredges, 110, 113, 155
drugs, 142 (*see also* medicine)

E
Echoes In the Wind, 66
Eckerd College, 20
eclipses, 152
education, 37, 85, 125, 150, 193–98 (*see also* schools *and* colleges *and* universitites)
egret plumes, 30, 55, 80
elders, 35, 37, 43, 47, 49, 81, 87, 112, 129, 177–78, 187, 195, 198
England, 3, 6–7, 73, 77, 145
Everglades, the, 1, 4, 13, 18–20, 27, 32–33, 40, 45–47, 62, 64, 85, 94, 96, 98–99, 102, 104-120, 126–27, 150, 155, 157, 161, 165, 169, 178
evil, 148, 180

F
faith, 140, 149 (*see also* God *and* religion)
federal (*see* U.S.)
Federal Preserve, 119
festivals, 140 (*see also* celebrations)
Fewell, Billy, 24 (*see also* Key West Billy)
fires, 68-69, 75, 81, 129, 133, 137-39 (*see also* cooking)
First Seminole Baptist Church, 37, 142
First Seminole Cavalry Battalion, 20
fish, 29, 33, 42, 65, 72, 75, 77, 94, 106, 109, 111, 113, 194
Fitzpatrick, Richard, 19

Flagler, Henry, 31
Fletcher, Senator Duncan Udall, 46
flintnapping, 173
Florida Baptist Institute, 24
Florida counties
  Alachua County, 6, 203
  Dade County, 99
  Hendry County, 194
  Sumter County, 12
  Volusia County, 6
Florida cracker, 101
Florida Folk Heritage Award, 95
Florida Historical Site, 109
Florida legislature, 10
Florida militia, 32
Florida panther, 114–18, 117, 205
Florida Women's Hall of Fame, 147
folklore, 210
food, 10, 47, 65–78, 106, 130, 134–35, 158, 175, 185
  frog legs, 65, 106, 158
  hearts of palm, 65, 76, 106
  swamp cabbage, 76
    See also beverages and plants.
Foosh Hatchet, 98
Forever Island, 105 (see also Smith, Patrick D.)
forts, 9–10, 12, 18–20
  Fort Brooke, 19, 52, 82
  Fort Dallas, 19–20
  Fort Drane, 12
  Fort King, 19, 50–51, 56
  Fort Lauderdale, 19
  Fort Marion, 14
  Fort Moultrie, 53
  Fort Myers, 19, 24
  Fort Peyton, 53
  Fort Pierce, 62, 108
  Fort Scott, 10
"Forty Mile Bend", 194
France, 123
Franciscans, 143
Frank, Joel, 69
Friends of the Seminoles, The, 96, 196

G

gambling, 143
games, 130, 132 (see also stickball)
gator (see alligator)
Glade Cross Episcopal Mission, 139
Glenn, James L., 62, 135, 195

God, 38, 42, 115, 117, 129–46, 150, 185 (see also Breathgiver; Breathmaker; and religion)
Gopher,
  Augustina, 186
  Jimmy, 148
  Louise, 188, 196
  John, 55
  John Henry, 38
gopher tortoise, 55, 71
government land, 15,112
grasshoppers, 151
graves, 51, 53, 131, 138–39, 144, 151 (see also ceremonies, burial)
Green Corn Dance, 49–50, 130–35
Grey Cloud, 30, 32
guides, 55–56

H

hair, 76, 79, 87, 137, 172, 177
half-breeds, 52, 137, 147
"Halpatachobee", 162
Halpatter Tustenuggee, 12 (see also Alligator)
hammocks, 18, 104
Hanson, Stanley W., 39, 46
Hard Rock Hotels/Casinos, 165
"Harmony", 104
Hartsuff, First Lieutenant George L., 16, 30
Hendi-La-Ma-La, 33 (see also Parker, Henry)
Hendry, Captain F. A., 24
Henry, Bobby, 94, 126–27
highways (see roads)
History of the Second Seminole War, 52
Holata Micco, 30
horses, 6, 11, 13–14, 18, 25, 137 (see also Marshtacky horse)
Huff, Sam, 97, 206
hunting, 1, 10, 26, 31, 33, 42, 51, 73, 79, 90, 94, 106, 109, 113, 119, 173, 194
hurricanes, 112

I

illnesses (see diseases and sicknesses)
Independent Traditional Seminole Nation, The, 41
Indian agents, 51, 193
Indian Home Guard, 30
Indian Medicine Lady, 148

Indian names, 78, 175, 177 (see also names)
Indian Removal Act of 1830, 11 (see also removal and Trail of Tears)
Indian Reorganization Act, 62
Indian Territory, 20
Indian wars, 56 (see also wars, Seminole Wars)
Indian Tribes (see Tribes)
Indian words/phrases
  afatchkee (happy)
  Ashawechobee (Big Cypress Reservation), 1, 158
  Atsi-na-hufa (Big Cypress Seminoles), 25
  Asiyaholo (black drink singer), 50, 205
  ayikomifo:si (medicine man), 24
  Che-he-cha-lah (See you later), 211
  chua (Newnan's Lake), 93
  ciki (house), 59
  Coontie hatchee (New River), 100
  Coowahchobee (Florida panther), 114
  Coyatalai (Pine Island), 109
  Eshocketomisee (white man's God), 144–45
  Eshocketomissee e-po-chee (Son of white man's God), 145
  Este Fasta (emissary), 135
  halpatee (alligator), 203
  hatchineha (cypress tree), 203
  hos-ko-ton-I (mosquitoes), 60
  Ikanyuksalgi (people of the peninsula), 205
  ichi bomet (Florida — the nose of the deer), 5
  I.laponki (Indians who speak Miccosukee [Hitchiti] language), 40
  isti siminoli (Seminoles), 5
  Kanyuksa (Florida), 1
  kishtubit (pestle), 65
  Oke-on-so-ho-ke-leica (Running Water City), 156
  Pahayokee (Everglades), 1
  Pithlachocco (place of long boats or place where boats are made), 93
  Pohapohumkosin (clan), 137
  Pohaan checkish ("Just leave us alone."), 16

Indian words/phrases, continued
   Shot Cay Taw (Green Corn
      Dance), 130
   taweekaache (patchwork clothing),
      82
   Watchie-estra/Hutrie (The Little
      White Mother), 196
   Wekiva (spring), 203
   See also languages.
Indigenous People, 117, 198 (*see also* Tribes)
internet, 165
interstate highways (*see* roads)

J

Jackson, Andrew (*see* United States, military forces, Generals of)
Jahvey, 144–45 (*see also* God)
Jaycees, 35
Jesus, 142, 144, 150 (*see also* Christianity)
jewelry, 30–31, 35, 58, 77, 79–80, 82, 122, 137, 158, 167, 173, 210 (*see also* beads)
Jim,
   Annie, 72
   April, 4
   Buffalo, 107
   Herbert, 4
   Mittie Osceola, 88–89
Jimmie,
   Ronnie, 6
   Annie, 47
   Annie Doctor, 89
John Family, 78
John,
   Doctor, 108
   Lena, 186
   Little, 185
   Lucy, 84
Johns, Edna, 186
Johnson, Cecil, 69–70
Jones,
   Rosemary E., 195
   Sam (Arpeika, Aviaka, Abiaki), 11, 51–52
Josh, Coleman, 194
Judaism, 135, 145
Jumper, 11–12, 36, 51
Jumper,
   Agnes, 68
   Alan, 165, 205
   Betty Mae, 27, 38, 81, 137, 147–48, 150, 172, 195 (*see also* Tiger, Betty Mae)
   Billie Tommie, 83
   Cathy, 209
   Cordell, 68
   Daniele, 125
   Desiree, 92
   Elsie, 164
   Holley, 38
   Holly, 164
   Henry, 88
   James, 68
   John, 20
   Josie, 97
   Moses, 104, 149
   Moses, Jr., 66
   Squirrel, 82–83, 88
   Tommie, 88
   Tommie Bert, 164
   Willie, 172
Jungle Queen boats, 157, 206

K

Key West Billy, 24
keys, 73
   Egmont Key, 33
   Indian Key, 9, 99
   Key West, 60
King,
   Willie, 141, 150
   Reverend, 141
Kiowa Indian Hospital, 148
kitchens, 65, 72 (*see also* cooking *and* fires)
Knight Sports Complex at the University of Miami, 97

L

LaBree, Guy, 101
lagoon of the Holy Spirit, 111
lakes, 93, 113
   Catfish Lake, 57
   Lake Apopka, 203
   Lake Hatchineha, 203
   Lake Miccosukee, 5
   Lake Okeechobee, 13, 15, 32–33, 57, 82, 112, 203
   Lake Pierce, 57
   Newnan's Lake, 93
languages, 23, 55, 85, 125, 140, 196
   ancient tongue, 130
   Arawak, 18
   classes for the Native, 196
   Creek, 193
   Hebrew, 144
   Hitchiti, 5–6, 40, 85, 193
   Maskoki, 5
   Miccosukee, 40, 193–94
   Muskogee, 6, 82, 193
Larkin, Mary Billie, 66
Lasher, Bert, 156
leaders, 2, 6, 7, 11, 13–14, 19, 36, 41, 46, 48–49, 51–52, 114, 133, 137, 142, 144, 147, 155, 195
legends, 29, 130, 147–54
   court-day legend, 134
   Legend of the Flood, The, 29
   Little People, 150
   Legend of the Panther and the Rattlesnake, The, 118
   Legend of the Rabbit and the Box Turtle, The, 153
lightning, 81, 121, 150
Little Bird, 140 (*see also* Bedell, Deaconess)
Little Mr. Seminole, 191
Little White Mother, The, 196
log cabins, 4, 59–60
loggers, 93, 112
Loomis, Colonel, 16
Louis, 56

M

McCall, Cristine, 92
McIver, Stuart, 195
McLaughlin, Lieutenant John T., 13
Ma-dee-lo-hee, 32 (*see also* Parker, Polly)
Madlow,
   John, 98
   John K., 52
   See also Motlow, John.
manatees, 73, 115
Marshtacky horse, 22 (*see also* horses)
matriarchs, 2, 45, 47, 75, 82, 125, 136, 194
Me-le, 84
medicine, 25, 32, 75, 87, 114–15, 121–24, 125–27, 133, 139, 142, 175, 210
medicine bundle, 114, 130, 133, 135
medicine men, 2, 11, 24, 28, 37, 45, 49, 94, 114, 121–28, 129, 131, 133–35, 139, 142, 147–48, 175, 179, 194

medicine pouch, 122
medicine women, 45, 121, 124, 129, 175
menopause, 121, 172
Mexico, 14, 144–45
Miami Historical Society, 189
Micanopah, 36 (see also Micanopy and Micco Nuppa)
Micanopy, 6, 11–12, 36, 51 (see also Micanopah and Micco Nuppa)
Micco Nuppa, 36 (see also Micanopah and Micanopy)
Miccosukee Tribe of Indians of Florida, 40, 210
Miccosukees, 24, 40–41, 60, 116, 193–94
Mikasuki, 59 (see also languages, Miccosukee)
Mikosuki, 82, 211 (see also languages, Miccosukee and Miccosukees)
Milky Way, 25
Miss Florida Seminole 2001, 92
Miss Florida Seminole 2005–2006, 92
Miss Teen Sugar, 92
Miss Universe contests, 159
missionaries, 139–41, 150, 193
Mitchell,
    Billy, 194
    Virginia, 68, 84–85, 177
Morning Dew, 50 (see also Chechoter)
Morrison, Virgil P., II, 22 (see also Swamp Owl)
Mosquito Fleet, 13, 16
mosquitoes, 6, 16, 60, 66, 80, 110–112, 126
Motlow,
    Bill, 123
    Billy, 168
    Jack, 63
    Jane, 81
    John, 98
    See also Madlow, John.
mound builders, 132
mud buggies, 119
music, 135, 149, 210 (see songs)
myths, 81, 147, 152 (see also legends and superstitions)

N

names, 134–35, 141, 145, 177 (see also Indian names)
National Museum of the American Indian, 21, 210
National Trust, 15
Native American lore, 174
Neamathla, 10
needles, 68, 134, 181
Nevaquaya, Sonny, 149
Newnan, Major Dan, 93
Niles National Register, 11
non-natives, 1, 24, 28, 70, 87, 101, 110, 114, 131, 141, 158, 175, 177, 182, 205 (see also whites)

O

Okaloacoochee Slough, 11
Okeechobee Battleground, 15
Old South Bar-B-Q Ranch, 159
Osceola, 11–12, 14, 50–53, 134, 197, 205 (see also Asiyahola! and Asiyaholo)
Osceola,
    Bill, 38
    Billy, 38, 44, 159
    Charlotte, 149 (see also Tommie, Mary)
    Cory 39, 48–49, 98, 109, 123, 164
    Dan, 38, 109
    Douglas, 41
    George, 190
    Guy, 42, 113
    Henehayo, 120
    Homer, 41
    Howard, 41, 149
    Huston, 191
    Jimmy O'Toole, 38
    Jimmy Scott, 194
    Joe Dan, 34–35, 38, 56, 60, 74, 81, 111, 131, 135, 141, 159, 195
    John, 41, 205
    Juanita, 49
    Laura Mae, 37–38, 82, 178, 185
    Mary, 86
    Mary Gay, 132
    Max, 38
    Mike, 39
    Nancy, 28, 179
    Robert, 130
    Shelli, 85
    Taham, 49
    Tihokee, 48
    William, 103
otters, 77, 106, 115

Otulke-thloco, 13

P

Parker, Henry 33 (see also Hendi-La-Ma-La)
Parker, Polly, 32–33 (see also Ma-dee-lo-hee)
parks
    Everglades National Park, 40
    Lummus Park, 19
    Payne's Prairie State Park, 7
Payne, King, 7
Payne's Landing, 36
Payne's Prairie, 6, 50, 203
Perrine, Dr., 111
Pilot, 125
plantations, 5, 7, 12, 56 (see also slaves)
plants, 210
    bananas, 30
    Brazilian pepper, 121
    cassina, 134
    coontie, 66, 100
    corn, 10, 65–66, 75, 130–31, 135
    ginseng, 134
    herbs, 121
    lizard's tail plant, 134
    myrsine plant, 44
    palmettos, 11, 13, 22, 59, 65, 76, 108, 138, 169, 171–72, 177
    poison ivy, 121
    pumpkins, 75
    sassafras, 121
    sawgrass, 13, 16, 33, 94, 106, 177
    shoestring fern, 121
    similax, 65
    snakeroot, 22, 134
    Spanish moss, 86–87
    strangler fig, 121
    sweet bay, 134
    sweet potatoes, 75
    sweetgrass, 169
    vegetables, 47
    zamia, 65
    See also beverages and food.
plumes, 30, 106, 155 (see also egret plumes)
points, 173 (see also weapons, arrowheads)
poling, 95–96, 98, 101, 106 (see also canoes)
politics, 149, 157
Post Office, 77
Powell, Billy, 50

powwows, 165
pregnancy, 175–76
Presidential Medal, 30
Puc-Puggy, 5 (*see also* Bartram, William)
punishments, 10, 130, 193
   banishment, 24, 134, 206
   cropping, 136
   ears cut off, 134
   ostracism, 24
   scratching, 68, 133–34, 181
   switching, 181
   whipping, 136
   See also needles.

R

R. R. Doubleday, 74
rabbits, 6–70, 153
railroads, 109, 206
rainmakers, 127
rattles, 130, 135
rattlesnakes, 82, 118, 133
re-enactments, 209
reclaimed land, 110 (*see also* Everglades, The)
Red Sticks, 9, 18 (*see also* Tribes, Creek, Upper Creek)
religion, 43, 107, 129–46, 194 (*see also specific religions*)
removal, 11, 13–14, 16, 20, 30, 33, 51, 60, 173, 193, 205 (*see also* Indian Removal Act of 1830 *and* Trail of Tears)
reservations, 1, 10–11, 34, 39, 42, 45, 62, 69, 100, 112, 124–25, 141–42, 174, 196
   Big Cypress Reservation, 11, 24, 80, 95, 100, 124–25, 142, 155, 158, 162, 165, 168, 194, 210
   Brighton Reservation, 57, 195–96
   Federal Reservation, 69
   Hollywood Reservation, 34, 165
   Miccossukee Reservation, 62
   Tampa Reservation, 127, 165
rituals, 135, 177 (*see also* ceremonies)
River of Grass, 105, 110 (*see also* Everglades, The)
rivers, 93, 113
   Apalachicola River, 9
   Fisheating Creek, 32, 57
   Kissimmee River, 32, 112
   Miami River, 19, 157
   New River, 100, 196, 206
   Oconee River, 6
   Oklawaha River, 203
   Peace River, 10
   River of Grass, 105, 110
   St. Marks River, 32
   Suwanee River, 5
   Tallapoosa River, 50
   Wekiwa River, 203
   Withlacoochee River, 12
   See also Everglades.
roads
   Broward Boulevard, 206
   Eighth Avenue, 206
   interstate highways, 157, 207
   Sterling Road, 34
   Tamiami Trail (U.S. Route 41), 39–41, 48, 62, 85, 96, 105–106, 127, 141–42, 165, 194
   Turner River road, 127
   U.S. Route 441, 34
Royal Palm Hammock, 88
Smith, Ruby, 87
Running Water City, 156 (*see also* Musa Isle)

S

schools, 10, 96, 143
   Afatchkee School, 194
   charter schools, 196
   Cherokee Indian School, 195
   curricula of, 196
   elementary schools, 194–96
   federal day school, 96
   high school, 148, 195–96
   middle school, 196
   Okeechobee County Schools, 195
   Okeechobee High School, 34
   public, 34, 85, 46, 195
   satellite schools, 196
   See also education *and* colleges *and* universitites.
scientists, 94, 116, 173
scouts, 20
Seaboard Coastline Railroad, 206
Seminole bands
   Alachua band, 6
   Cow Creek Seminoles, 32, 57, 62
   Fort Lauderdale Band of Seminoles, 46
   Fort Pierce group, 33
Seminole Club, 204
Seminole Days, 85
Seminole Music, 29
Seminole Tribal Fair, 172
Seminole Tribe of Florida, 11, 40, 210
   businesses of the
      cattle business, 199-202
      casinos, 165
      vegetable business, 106
   Chairman of the, 21, 44, 49, 147, 159
   Color Guard of the, 20–21
   constitution of the, 37
   Education Program of the, 196
   headquarters of the, 62
   Historical Society of the, 34
   See also tourist attractions.
Seminole Tribune, 84–85, 92, 142
Seminole Village in Hollywood, 130
Seminole Wars (*see* wars, Seminole Wars)
sequence of fours, 143
sewing, 60, 81, 84 (*see also* clothing, patchwork)
Shirt-tail Charlie, 206
Shirt-tail Charlie's, 206
Shoe,
   Brown, 194
   Eddy, 194
Sholtz, Florida Governor David, 39
Shore
   Jim, 195
   Lottie 67
sicknesses, 67, 121–22, 126 (*see also* diseases)
Silver, Morton, 38
slaves, 6–7, 10, 12, 19, 36, 50, 56 (*see also* Blacks *and* plantations)
Smallwood, Ted, 77–78
Smallwood's Store, 77 (*see also* tourist attractions)
Smith,
   Lieutenant, 51
   Patrick D., 105, 132, 169, 203
   Richard, 194
   The Reverend Stanley, 141
Smithsonian, The, 125
snakes, 14, 16, 59, 133, 181
Snow, Alice, 72
songs, 75, 104, 121, 123, 126–27, 131, 149 (*see also* chants)
souls, 126, 129, 139, 142, 144
Southern Association of Colleges and Schools, 194

Southern Baptist Convention, 141
Spain, 5–7, 10, 19, 56, 111, 123
Spencer, Lucien A., 46, 195
spirits, 6, 33, 53, 75, 114, 131, 137, 142, 144
squaws, 28, 90, 177, 189
State of Florida, 20, 119, 208
states
  Alabama, 3, 5–6, 18
  Arkansas, 32
  Carolinas, 5, 7, 55
    North Carolina, 148
    South Carolina, 6, 14, 18, 53
  Georgia, 3–7, 9–10, 18, 50, 55, 82, 126, 173
  Missouri, 13
  Oklahoma, 14, 141, 148, 173, 205
  Virginia, 34, 203
  West Virginia, 69
  See also cities *by state.*
stickball, 131–32
storytellers, 184
Stranahan & Co. Trading Post, 195
Stranahan, Frank and Ivy, 46, 95–96, 193, 195–96, 206
Stranahan House, Frank and Ivy Stanahan: New River Pioneers, 195
Stuart, John, 5
Superman, 162
superstitions, 175
swamps, 10–13, 16, 18, 22, 32, 82, 113, 116, 124, 210
  Big Cypress Swamp, 1, 165
  Great Wahoo Swamp, 56
  Okefinokee Swamp, 82
swamp buggies, 119, 158
Swamp Owl, 22 (*see also* Morrison, Virgil P., II)

T
Tallahassee Tustenuggee, 50
Tamiami Canal, 112
Tampa Bay, 6 (*see also* cities, Florida, Tampa)
tattoos, 159
Taylor, Colonel Zachary, 13
thatching, 59, 60, 76 (*see also* chickees)
Thompson, Agent Wiley, 50–51
"The Prophet", 55 (*see also* Cavillo, John)
thunder, 150, 180

thunder missile, 133
Thunderbird Indian Trading Post, 174
Tiger Family, 205 (*see also* individual Tiger Family members)
Tiger,
  Ada, 68, 171
  Annie, 181
  Betty Mae, 147–50, 195
  Bobby, 41, 205, 181
  Buffalo, 38, 40–41, 170
  Charlie, 134
  Desoto, 27
  Doctor, 39, 98
  Effie, 28
  Emma, 75
  Eugene, 102
  Howard, 20
  Jane, 63
  Janette, 194
  Jimmy, 38, 141
  Jo Jo, 181, 205
  Josie, 41
  Louis, 181
  Mary Gopher, 148
  Micky, 89, 205
  Mickey, 72
  Naha, 26
  Pauline, 75
  Sally, 72
  Tom, 27
  Tommy, 41, 141, 205
Tigertail,
  Bobby, 102
  Jack, 205
toads, 152
tobacco, 17, 96, 108, 135
Tommie Family, 77, 135
Tommie,
  Annie, 45–46, 61, 171
  Danny, 116, 119
  Frank, 97
  Howard, 172
  Mary, 149 (*see also* Osceola, Charlotte)
  Sally Chupco, 13
  Sally, 13, 33, 47, 137, 198
  Samuel, 209
  Tony, 46, 206
tourist attractions, 40, 48, 61–62, 77, 105, 130, 140–41, 155–66, 168, 172–74, 181
  airboat rides, 40, 102–103, 158, 165

  alligator farms, 161
  alligator wrestling, 149, 156, 158, 160–61, 163–166
  Billie Swamp Safari, 100, 155, 158, 162, 165
  Buffalo Tiger's Florida Everglades Airboat Rides, 40
  Coppinger's Pirate Cove, 157
  ecotourism, 165
  gift shops, 48, 123, 158, 174
  Howard Tommie's smoke shop, 172
  Musa Isle, 41, 48–49, 72, 89, 155–57, 164, 166, 170, 188
  Smallwood's Store, 77, 95
  swamp buggy rides, 158
  Swamp Water Café, 158
  Willie Jumper's cold drink stand, 172
  See also Everglades, the; gift shops; *and* trading posts.
trading posts, 62, 77–78, 90, 96, 106, 174, 196
traditionalists, 41–42, 112, 141
traditions, 42, 47, 62, 65, 75, 87–88, 90, 95, 122, 125, 130–31, 137, 140, 176, 184, 193–94, 210
Trail of Tears, 33 (*see also* removal)
Travels and Other Writings, 79
treaties, 10, 51
Treaty of Moultrie Creek, 10
trees, 76, 81, 104, 112, 118, 121, 134, 150 (*see also* cypress)
Tribes
  Ais', 3
  Aztec, 144–45
  Apalachee, 3, 5–6
  Apalachicola, 5
  Calusa, 3, 4, 59, 89
  Cherokee, 147
  Chiaha, 5
  Choctaw, 10, 147
  Commanche, 14
  Creek, 3–7, 10, 141, 145, 193
    Lower Creek, 3, 5–6, 18
    Upper Creek, 3, 6, 9, 18
  Delaware, 10
  Eufaula, 6
  Independent Seminole, 2, 194
  Independent Traditional Seminole Nation of Florida, 43, 210
  Independent Traditional Seminole, 39

Tribes, continued
  Kickapoo, 10, 14
  Matacumbe, 3
  Mescalero Apaches, 14
  Miccosukee, 24, 60, 82, 85, 109, 125, 147, 210–11
  Miccosukee Tribe of Indians of Florida, 40, 210
  Muskogee, 5–6, 65, 82, 145, 193
  Muskogee Seminole, 193
  Oconee, 6, 122
  Saulk, 10
  Shawnee, 10
  Tallassees, 6
  Tamothli, 5
  Timacuan, 3
  Tocobaga, 3
  Yamassee, 137
  Yemassee, 3, 6
  Yuchi, 6
  See also Seminole Tribe of Florida.
turtles, 65, 68–71, 73, 77, 81, 130, 135, 153
Twigs, Major David, 10

U

United States, 1, 7, 16, 18, 21, 193
  Army, 10, 12–13, 18–19, 21, 53
  Army Corps of Engineers, 111
  Indian aid from the, 41
  Congress, 62
  military forces of the, 4–5, 9–13, 18–21, 30, 52, 56, 60, 177
    Generals of
      General Clinch, 12, 36
      General Gaines, 10
      General Andrew Jackson, 6, 9-11
      General Thomas S. Jesup, 11, 16, 52, 111
    Marine Corps, 13, 16, 20
    Navy, 13, 16, 20
    veterans of the, 21
  government of the, 1, 5, 11, 16, 18, 38–40, 59–60, 113, 144
  officials of the, 52, 62
  Presidents of the
    Adams, John Quincy, 10
    Cleveland, Grover, 210
    Coolidge, Calvin, 46
    Polk, James, 19
    Tyler, John, 20
    Filmore, Millard, 30
  Senate of the, 11
  Supreme Court of the, 10
  Vice-Presidents of the
    Dallas, George Mifflin, 19
Union Army, 20, 30 (*see also* wars, Civil War)
United Nations, 41
United Southeastern Tribes, 34, 147
universities (*see also* colleges)
  Florida State University, 147, 197, 203
  logos of, 197
  mascots of, 197
  University of Florida, 97
  University of Miami, 97
Upjohn Pharmaceutical Company, 126

V

vermillion paint, 159
villages, 6, 10, 19, 42, 63–64, 85, 94, 105, 130, 133, 139 (*see also* camps)

W

war speaker, 133
warriors, 2, 9–14, 16–17, 20–21, 27, 55, 57, 122, 133–34
wars, 9–22, 60, 90, 114, 131, 133
  Civil War, 20, 30, 56, 137
  Creek War, 9
  Dade Massacre, 12, 39
  Red-Stick War, 6
  Revolutionary War, 7
  Seminole Wars, 5–6, 12–13, 16, 18–19, 55, 131, 133, 177, 193
    First Seminole War, 4, 9
    Second Seminole War, 12, 14, 50, 52, 57
    Third Seminole War, 16, 30, 32, 45
  World War I, 82, 106
  World War II, 33, 149, 195
  See also battles.
ways of conduct, 184
weapons
  arrowheads, 173
  bows and arrows, 14, 44, 138, 173
  guns, 94, 96, 136, 139
  knives, 51, 96
  rifles, 147
  spears, 173
  words as, 18

Wekiwa, 203 (*see also* Indian names, Wekiva)
West Indies, 65
whites, 5–7, 9, 12, 14, 19, 40, 42, 48–51, 57, 65, 75, 77–78, 94–95, 106, 112–13, 123, 136–37, 139, 141, 144, 187–88, 193–95, 205 (*see also* non-natives)
  cheating Seminoles, 1, 10, 127, 153
  harassing the Seminoles, 19
  medicine of the, 127, 148
  persecution of Seminoles by, 1, 16, 21, 33, 56, 211
  trickery of the, 11, 156
Wildcat, 12, 14, 52, 55, 180 (*see also* Coacoochee)
English, William, 19
Willie Family, 186
Willie,
  Charlie, 186
  Mrs. Charlie, 58
  Frank, 186
  Jackie, 38
  John, 123
  Martha, 84–85
  Sam, 85
  Willie, 156
wolves, 14, 52
Worth, Colonel, 14

Y

yat'siminoli, 5
Yucatan peninsula, 144
Yupefushket, 89

About the Author

Emmett H. L. Snellings, Jr., received his master's degree from George Mason University in Fairfax, Virginia, in 1993. Upon the acceptance of his master's thesis, a new genre in literature was established — the environmental/historical novel. The text used to establish this was Patrick Smith's novel, *A Land Remembered*. His thesis is on record with the Nobel Library in Stockholm, Sweden. During the last thirty years Emmett has had many articles and papers, on a wide variety of subjects, published in various publications throughout the United States. Interested in Native American culture since he was a boy, Emmett sought to promote their uniqueness with *Seminole Views*.

E
99
.S28
S645
2008